the Developing Brain

This book is dedicated to Adam, Alayna, Benjamin, Jenna, Jordan, Matthew, Noah, and especially to Jackson Joseph Sprenger and his anxiously awaited baby sister!

the Developing
Brain

Birth to Age Eight

Marilee Sprenger

CORWIN PRESS
A SAGE Company
Thousand Oaks, CA 91320

For information:

Corwin Press
A SAGE Company
2455 Teller Road
Thousand Oaks, California 91320
www.corwinpress.com

SAGE Ltd.
1 Oliver's Yard
55 City Road
London EC1Y 1SP
United Kingdom

SAGE India Pvt. Ltd.
B 1/I 1 Mohan Cooperative
    Industrial Area
Mathura Road, New Delhi 110 044
India

SAGE Asia-Pacific Pte. Ltd.
33 Pekin Street #02-01
Far East Square
Singapore 048763

Printed in the United States of America.

Library of Congress Cataloging-in-Publication Data

Sprenger, Marilee, 1949-
The developing brain: birth to age eight/Marilee Sprenger.
    p. cm.
Includes bibliographical references and index.
ISBN 978-1-4129-5534-8 (cloth)
ISBN 978-1-4129-5535-5 (pbk.)
    1. Developmental neurobiology. 2. Child development. I. Title.

QP363.5.S67 2008
612.8—dc22   2007043469

This book is printed on acid-free paper.

08   09   10   11   12   10 9 8 7 6 5 4 3 2 1

Acquisitions Editor:	Hudson Perigo
Editorial Assistant:	Lesley K. Blake
Production Editor:	Eric Garner
Copy Editor:	Cate Huisman
Typesetter:	C&M Digitals (P) Ltd.
Proofreader:	Kevin Gleason
Indexer:	Sheila Bodell
Cover Designer:	Scott Van Atta

Contents

Preface

I have always liked my men tall, dark, and handsome. I never thought I'd fall for a short, bald guy. But here I am in love. With Jack. He has blue eyes and pretty sparse light brown hair. When he smiles at me, he makes me the happiest woman alive . . . even though he is missing many teeth. Not a tall guy, Jack stands at about 32 inches.

Yes, I am finally in a club I couldn't wait to join. I am a grandmother.

From the moment my daughter-in-law Amy and my son Josh became pregnant I couldn't stop thinking about . . . this baby's brain. I started my career teaching prekindergarten and kindergarten, but since then I have taught at all levels. I have been immersed in brain research as it has so miraculously unfolded over the past 20 years. I have translated it for educators and applied it at all levels. But this pregnancy caused me to take a closer look at the brain as it develops. And I am amazed.

There has been much research of late about the adolescent brain. I voraciously read the research and have shared my reactions, applications, and suggestions to teachers and parents all over the world. In writing my books, I have covered brain development. But there were always pieces missing. It seems that some information about brain development from birth to age three was available, and then most of the literature jumped to the adolescent brain. What was happening really between birth and eight? The literature would read, "From the terrible twos, when the child has an abundance of connections, pruning begins to take place." The next thing I knew, I was reading about puberty!

After hearing the exciting news of the pregnancy, I knew I had to find whatever information was available about those missing years. Since then, I have been reviewing the research on early brain development and its implications. I have gathered information from neuroscience, cognitive psychology, and child development and have been able to outline the brain's development from birth through adolescence. From attending conferences on the brain in early childhood to having personal conversations with some of the well-known early childhood experts, I have learned fascinating things.

We have all read about the importance of the first three years. I will describe those ages of development along with behaviors and suggestions, and then I will focus on the ages from three through eight. Why? This is when most children come in contact with educators. These are the ages for which public and private education must design appropriate curricula. These are the ages when teachers can begin to make a difference.

As teachers, we have the unique and overwhelming responsibility of changing children's brains on a daily basis. We have the opportunity to take children from varied backgrounds and nurture them. We have the power to influence the development of successful people who are enlightened citizens and caring individuals.

Time and again the research has shown us that development is a combination of nature and nurture. DNA provides the blueprint that the brain will follow as it unravels its mysteries, and we can provide the nurturing to make the most of its development.

As the neuroscientists who wrote *The Scientist in the Crib* (Gopnik, Meltzoff, & Kuhl, 1999) so eloquently state,

> Nurture is our nature, and the drive to learn is our most important instinct.

In this book you will get to know Jack and other young children as they grow and develop. I will provide you with a design of how the brain develops at each age level. Keep in mind two things:

1. Children grow at individual paces. There can be a large variance in brain development.

2. Boys and girls develop differently. Brain development in girls is generally faster than in boys, just as their physical development is accelerated.

I have provided you with the best research that I have been able to acquire. There are many researchers responsible for this new area of understanding. I am so appreciative of the work of the following experts: Harriett Arnold, Laura Berk, Maurice Elias, Lise Eliot, Alison Gopnik, Jane Healy, Elinore Chapman Herschkowitz, Norbert Herschkowitz, Jerome Kagan, Andrew Meltzhoff, Patricia Kuhl, Chip Wood, the National Research Council Institute of Medicine, and the American Academy of Pediatrics. There are many more neuroscientists, cognitive psychologists, and child development experts working in the area of early childhood. The National Association for the Education of Young Children works diligently to provide information to help all young children learn.

I also want to thank my colleagues who interpret the research. By sharing and comparing, we try to present the best applications possible. I am especially grateful to Carla Hannaford, Eric Jensen, Kathy Nunley, David Sousa, Robert Sylwester, Donna Tileston, Pat Wolfe, and Rick Wormeli.

This book would not have been possible without the guidance of Faye Zucker, Stacy Wagner, and my new editor, Hudson Perigo. These professionals along with their excellent staff provided gentle guidance through the process of writing this book.

I hope you find this to be a sensible guide to help you understand the students in your classroom and to help you design the best learning experiences possible.

No, you don't know Jack, but you soon will!

Acknowledgments

Corwin Press gratefully acknowledges the contributions of the following people:

Linda Brault
Early Childhood Special Education
    Consultant
Director of Statewide Training &
    Technical Assistance Projects
Oceanside, CA

Stacey B. Ferguson
National Board Certified Teacher
North Bay Elementary School
Bay St. Louis, MS

Laura Linde
Literacy Coach
Hoover Elementary School
North Mankato, MN

Stephanie Malin
Elementary Instructional Coach
Beaverton School District
Beaverton, OR

Miranda Moe
Elementary Teacher/New Teacher
    Facilitator
Beaver Dam Unified School District
Sun Prairie, WI

Nathan Naparstek
Psychologist
Schenectady City Schools and
    Northeast Psychological Associates
Schenectady, NY

Gail Underwood
Math Coach
Columbia Public Schools
Columbia, MO

About the Author

Marilee Sprenger began her teaching career as a prekindergarten and kindergarten teacher. Since then she has taught at the elementary, middle, and high school levels. She is considered an expert in education on the brain, learning, and memory. She is one of the most entertaining and informative authors and speakers in the field of education. She leaves her audiences with practical techniques to implement in their classrooms immediately.

Marilee is a member of the American Academy of Neurology as well as many education organizations, such as the Association for Supervision and Curriculum Development and Phi Delta Kappa. She is the author of *Learning and Memory: The Brain in Action*, *Becoming a "Wiz" at Brain-Based Teaching*, *Differentiation Through Learning Styles and Memory*, *How to Teach So Students Remember*, and *Memory 101 for Educators*. She has written numerous articles, contributes to textbooks, and provides staff development internationally.

She is an adjunct professor at Aurora University, teaching graduate courses on brain-based teaching, learning and memory, and differentiation. Teachers who have read Marilee's work or heard her speak agree that they walk away with user-friendly information that can be applied at all levels.

You can reach her at
5820 North Briarwood Lane
Peoria, IL 61614
Phone: (309) 692-5820
Email: brainlady@gmail.com
Web sites: www.brainlady.com
www.marileesprenger.com

Introduction

Cal arrived at school each day on the bus. It took almost an hour for this kindergartner to get to school from his home in the housing projects on the south side of town. About 16 percent of the students at his school were bussed in.

There were few books in Cal's home, and he never saw anyone in his family read. When he first picked up a book at school, he held it upside down. Stephen was sitting next to Cal in the book corner. He called Cal "stupid" and took the book out of his hands. Stephen turned the book around and shoved it back at him. Cal was shocked but mostly angry. He pushed Stephen to the ground. This time Stephen was the one who was shocked.

These two boys from dissimilar backgrounds had different experiences. Stephen knew how to hold a book. He had seen every member of his family read and had been read to often. Cal knew how to fight. He was always shown that you were weak if you didn't defend yourself.

Their kindergarten teacher had her work cut out for her. By the end of the year, Cal was reading books. Stephen learned to be careful around kids like Cal, but Cal also learned that he didn't have to defend himself physically.

Two critical areas of research in the neurosciences are influencing how we educate our young children. The first significant subject of research is referred to as *plasticity*. Plasticity is the link between nature and nurture. Mental and physical activity stimulates physiological and structural changes in the brain. These changes are mediated by gene expression and facilitate learning (Begley, 2007). In other words, experience changes the brain. The experiences we provide all children will affect their very brain structure. Both Cal's and Stephen's brains changed during their year in kindergarten.

The second area of research is the startling discovery of "mirror neurons." These are networks in the premotor area of the brain that fire when we watch someone else do something. They fire in the same way that they would if we were performing the action ourselves. This implies that when a child watches an adult do something, a network begins firing in the brain. (A simple example of this is our inclination to yawn when someone else does so.) Empathy, language, and social behavior may center on what a child sees. These mirror neurons may be capable of encoding not just the movements, but also the motive behind the movement. Handling books had been modeled for Stephen; his brain was wired for managing books before he got to school. Cal's brain had watched a lot of fighting. His brain was wired differently.

Therefore, the experiences we make available and the modeling we do will affect the brains of our students. The primary reason for this book is to provide the knowledge to create appropriate curricula for our young children. By understanding their developmental phases and brain growth, we can decide what to do in the classroom to meet the children on their level and help them move on to the next. Cognitive development, language development, social development, and physical development are all components of learning.

WHAT IS BEST PRACTICE?

Brain-Compatible Teaching Principles

The brain is the only organ in the body that is shaped through its interaction with the environment. If the brain is the organ that is dedicated to learning and memory, educators need to be familiar with brain-compatible practices and those that are brain antagonistic. Based on what we currently know about the structure and function of the brain, brain-compatible teaching emphasizes the way the brain naturally learns.

In my own personal journey toward brain-based teaching, I practice the following principles as the basis for best practice.

1. **Every brain is totally unique.** There will never be two children in your classroom who learn in exactly the same way. Some of this is genetics, and the rest is experience. Therefore, we must offer a variety of approaches to learning.

2. **Emotions guide our learning.** The emotional brain filters all incoming information. If it is emotionally stimulating, it will be marked for memory. The emotions that our children feel when they enter the classroom also affect how well they will learn. The more positive the emotions are, the more likely the children will learn. The more positive the teacher is, the more likely the students will be positive, because emotions are contagious!

3. **Stress affects learning.** A little bit of stress sends out chemicals to make us more alert and help us remember. Chronic stress or acute stress sends out more chemicals that interfere with learning. Creating an environment that keeps stress levels low might include using soothing music, offering choices, and providing predictability.

4. **There is a brain-body connection.** What our students eat, how much they sleep, whether they exercise, and the amount of movement we offer in the classroom all affect what is happening in their brains.

5. **The brain has multiple memory systems and multiple modalities.** According to neuroscientist Dr. Steve Peterson (2001), these two pieces of information suggest strong recommendations for the classroom. The more systems and modalities we utilize for learning, the stronger the possibility of receiving and retrieving the information. With those unique brains, there are students who have difficulty with one system and do better with another (Sprenger, 2006).

6. **The brain seeks meaning and relevance.** It is vital that we teach children that which is important to them. If something does not make sense, the brain will drop it. Showing students how information will be used outside the classroom will help them make sense of it.

7. **The brain learns through experience.** Hands-on activities, role-playing, field trips, and simulations all enhance the learning experience.

8. **The brain is social.** Brains learn best with other brains. Cooperative learning is one of the nine strategies that raise student achievement (Marzano, Pickering, & Pollack, 2001).

9. **The brain learns in patterns.** New information that can be connected to a pattern of stored information is more easily remembered. Pattern recognition is our ability to take in and make sense of our environment. There are patterns in objects, actions, procedures, situations, relationships, and systems. (A young child drinks from a glass. Later she sees a small empty vase and picks it up and tries to drink from it.)

10. **The brain grows through enrichment.** Appropriate challenges, choices, novelty, and feedback all add to the enrichment experience.

Early Childhood Principles

According to the National Association for the Education of Young Children, the following 12 principles inform best practice when dealing with young children (National Association for the Education of Young Children, 1996).

1. **Domains of children's development—physical, social, emotional, and cognitive—are closely related. Development in one domain influences and is influenced by development in other domains.** Curriculum and teaching strategies should be organized in such a way that these domains are included in every aspect. The suggested developmentally appropriate strategies in each chapter of this book are categorized, yet they relate to the other domains as well.

2. **Development occurs in a relatively orderly sequence, with later abilities, skills, and knowledge building on those already acquired.** Just as children walk before they run, there are many readiness skills for reading and math. Children want and need the opportunity to practice their skills past perfection, so these skills become automatic and can be relied upon without much or any conscious processing. In this way, the brain has space and energy to apply new information to the old.

3. **Development proceeds at varying rates from child to child as well as unevenly within different areas of each child's functioning.** Because Jack isn't speaking the way his friend Madonna is doesn't mean that Jack is behind. One must consider gender differences, differences in experience, and what domain Jack is concentrating on. If his brain is busy practicing motor skills, it may not have the time and energy to work on speech. Once he has perfected some of his physical skills, he will work on other domains.

4. **Early experiences have both cumulative and delayed effects on individual children's development; optimal periods exist for certain types of development and learning.** Some children do not have the opportunities that others do. Children from poverty may have delayed development due to poor nutrition, lack of sleep, or lack of role models.

5. **Development proceeds in predictable directions toward greater complexity, organization, and internalization.** The brain develops from back to front. Children start with motor skills and sensory skills, and it is not until the frontal lobe makes enough connections that higher-level thinking takes place.

6. **Development and learning occur in and are influenced by multiple social and cultural contexts.** The brain learns through experience. The physical, emotional, and cognitive environment all influence learning and development. Our students come from varying cultures. It behooves us to learn about and understand these cultures in order to help our students learn and grow.

7. **Children are active learners, drawing on direct physical and social experience as well as culturally transmitted knowledge to construct their own understandings of the world around them.** The brain seeks meaning. That meaning will be based on the brain's background and experiences. Making learning relevant to our students is one of our biggest challenges. What is meaningful to one child may not be meaningful to another.

8. **Development and learning result from interaction of biological maturation and the environment, which includes both the physical and social worlds that children live in.** By making yourself aware of brain biology and brain development you can be better prepared to teach the way your students' brains learn.

9. **Play is an important vehicle for children's social, emotional, and cognitive development as well as a reflection of their development.** Play is included in the developmentally appropriate activities at every level of early childhood. Children learn implicitly through play. Implicit learning is longer lasting than most explicit learning.

10. **Development advances when children have opportunities to practice newly acquired skills as well as when they experience a challenge just beyond the level of their present mastery.** The brain loves repetition and challenge. Teachers must act as coaches as their students meet new challenges. It is through trial and error learning that the brain learns what is important to focus upon.

11. **Children demonstrate different modes of knowing and learning and different ways of representing what they know.** The brain is multimodal. It expresses itself in a multimodal fashion and it receives information through multiple senses.

12. **Children develop and learn best in the context of a community where they are safe and valued, their physical needs are met, and they feel psychologically secure.** The brain learns best when learning with other brains. Safety and predictability allow the brain to have lower levels of stress chemicals that may interfere with learning.

AN OUNCE OF PREVENTION

According to the National Association for the education of Young Children, early childhood begins at birth. The achievement gap can also begin then. What does a child need to have an even start? The McCormick Tribune Foundation has a ten-point list of what can boost brain power (McCormick Tribune Foundation, 1997).

1. **Interaction:** The brain is social. Interaction makes children feel that they are worth spending time with.

2. **Loving Touch:** The body thrives with touch. Greeting students at the door, addressing them by name, and touching their shoulders or shaking their hands can make a difference. Young children need lots of hugs.

3. **Stable Relationship:** Everyone needs a significant other in his or her life. If there is no one at home to give a child a stable relationship, you might be the one!

4. **Safe, Healthy Environment:** At home, this means keeping dangerous items out of the way, protecting children from lead, and giving them proper nutrition. At school, we can support good nutrition, offer them a safe environment, and help them feel like they belong.

5. **Self-Esteem:** Offering children positive reinforcement, appropriate feedback, and giving them doable challenges can help them feel good about themselves.

6. **Quality Child Care:** This must be provided by people who can be trusted by parent and child. Providers must be aware of human development and the needs that children have.

7. **Communication:** The more children are spoken to, the more they will understand. From listening comes speaking, and from speaking comes reading.

8. **Play:** Play is learning, and this kind of learning is fun. Brains want to learn and they want to have fun. One study found that children deprived of playtime at school developed ADHD symptoms. They had difficulty sitting still and could not focus their attention (Sunderland, 2006).

9. **Music:** Music provides patterns for the brain. It also affects mood and movement. For those children who are stressed, music can help them relax.

10. **Reading:** Read to children every day. Show pictures and let them make up stories. Write their stories down and show them how their words can become a story.

About This Book

What you will find in Chapter 1 of this book is background information about how the brain grows. Pertinent structures and functions are all defined for you, so that when these terms appear in subsequent chapters, you will have the background knowledge you need. This may be a refresher for some of you, so feel free to skip the chapter and go back to it if a question arises while you read the rest of the book.

Chapter 2 covers birth through the end of the second year. This is background for you as you read Chapters 3–8, which provide year-by-year child and brain development. Each of these chapters begins with a scenario of a child. This will give you an overall snapshot of the age level. Then you will read about the latest applications of research about the developing brain for that age. Reading and language developmental milestones follow. Language and literacy skills will affect both personal and school success. Physical development and motor skills are next and become even more important as research suggests the strong connection between movement and learning. Cognitive development will offer information on learning and memory. Social/emotional development affects every aspect of a child's life. Becoming familiar with these milestones will help in planning curriculum and instruction. How children progress in their personal relationships will influence their learning (Jacobs & Crowley, 2007). There are sample activities at the end of each chapter that are developmentally appropriate for the age group. Please remember that if you are teaching four-year-olds, you may easily have brains that are a year or two behind or a year or two ahead.

> ### Brain Briefing
>
> The boxes throughout the text provide added information. *They are not pullouts from the text.* These are bits of research to support the text and to add to your knowledge base. I hope you find them interesting and helpful.

Child development books offer you guidelines and possibilities. I cannot stress how important it is that we understand that all brains are different. If you use the information in this book or any other as a yardstick, someone is going to come up short. These are child and brain development phases rather than stages. We all like to put ages and stages together in a nice neat package. Children don't come with a user's manual. Look at the big picture. You will be teaching 10 to 20 (or more) students at one time. Their chronological ages will differ. Their brain ages will differ. Their genders will differ. Their parents will differ. Their background knowledge . . . need I go on? The ages given for milestones are determined by the age at which 90 percent of children have achieved the objective. If a baby has been born prematurely, up until age two you must adjust the age by subtracting the number of months missed during pregnancy (Fields & Brown, 2006). It is impossible to include every potential behavior at any stage of development. What you will read are composite lists from the experts in their fields. The suggested developmentally appropriate activities are from my own experiences, from practitioners like you, and from child development experts. At the end of each chapter is a checklist that you can copy and use for each student. This is to help you determine what you need to consider when designing instruction and the physical environment.

You have the awesome responsibility of offering experiences to shape growing brains. Every day when you walk into your classroom, there are brains seeking learning. By understanding and teaching the way the brain learns best, you can stimulate an enduring love of learning.

My hope is that this information will also be used to enlighten the parents of your students as they watch the incredible development of their children!

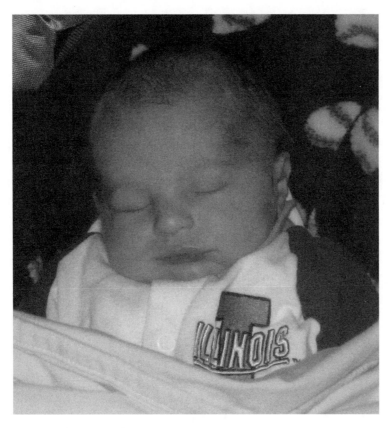

Figure 1.1   Matthew: Newborn

The Basic Biology of Brain Development

The brain is without doubt our most fascinating organ. Parents, educators, and society as a whole have a tremendous power to shape the wrinkly universe inside each child's head, and, with it, the kind of person he or she will turn out to be. We owe it to our children to help them grow the best brains possible.

—L. Eliot (1999)

> ### *Brain Briefing*
>
> Although the brain is the least developed organ at birth, the baby has already started making connections to Mom through both smell and sound (Rodriguez, 2007).

Brain development begins shortly after conception. Yes, Jack's brain was busily creating itself from what is called the neural tube (Figure 1.2). This tube closed after about three weeks of gestation and proceeded to form itself into the miraculous structure we call the brain. Neurogenesis, the birth of neurons, proceeds rapidly. Since a baby is born with 100 billion neurons, they must be growing at a rate of over half a million per minute! (Eliot, 1999)

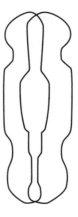

Figure 1.2   The Neural Tube That Will Form Into the Central Nervous System

The neural tube is made up of cells that will give rise to the central nervous system. There are two different types of cells of which to be aware. **Neurons** are the brain cells that do most of the communicating in the brain and that we associate most with learning. **Glial** cells are support cells. They remove unneeded debris, and some literally wrap themselves around the output fiber of the neuron known as the **axon**. This white, sticky wrapper is called the **myelin sheath**. Myelin reinforces this message-sending appendage so that information moves faster and more securely. Besides having an axon that can send messages, neurons have **dendrites** to receive messages. Dendrites are the fibers that receive the information that has been sent out through another neuron's axon. Remember: In through the dendrite; out through the axon! (Figure 1.3)

So, here we are with this teeny brain developing from the embryonic stage through the fetal stage. As the brain forms from the neural tube, neurons **migrate** to specific areas to learn to perform interesting tasks. For instance, some go to the occipital lobe in the back of the brain and become visual neurons. It is during this

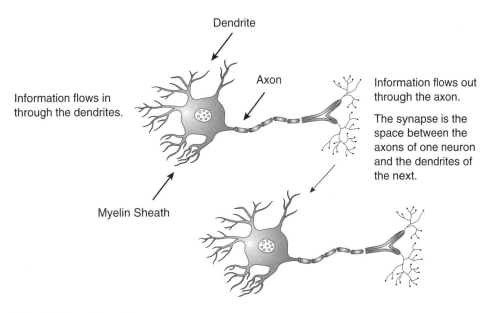

Figure 1.3   Neuron

migration that the brain is highly susceptible to toxins such as alcohol. A pregnant woman drinking alcohol at crucial times can cause the neurons to change their migratory pattern. One result of this can be fetal alcohol syndrome.

These brain cells migrate to become specific structures in the brain, from the brain stem that receives incoming sensory information (except for the sense of smell) all the way up to the neocortex that does our higher levels of thinking. The neocortex, also called the cerebral cortex, makes up about 80 percent of the brain's volume (Figure 1.4). It is the outer layer of the brain that we sometimes call our gray matter.

Beneath the neocortex is a subcortical area called the limbic system. It consists of the thalamus, hypothalamus, hippocampus, and amygdala. The hypothalamus deals with internal communication between the body and the

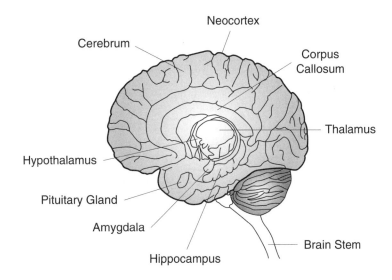

Figure 1.4   View of the Brain

brain. The thalamus is a relay station for incoming information. It sends the messages to the appropriate places in the brain.

In particular we will follow the growth of

- the **hippocampus,** which helps us form long-term factual memories.
- the **amygdala,** which filters all incoming information for emotional content.
- the **corpus callosum,** which connects the two hemispheres of the brain.

The brain is divided into a left and a right hemisphere. The hemispheres work together, yet each has some specific functions. Table 1.1 lists the information processing functions of each. Emotions and reading are just two areas that depend on the connections or "cross-talk" of these hemispheres (Elias & Arnold, 2006; Kagan & Herschkowitz, 2004).

Table 1.1 Functions of the Two Hemispheres Help Us Determine Specific Child Development Growth as the Two Hemispheres Grow and Connect

Left Hemisphere	Right Hemisphere
Logical	Holistic
Details	Big picture
Language: speech, grammar, sounds Expressive and receptive language	Language: prosody, tone
Verbal short-term memory	Sensory image memory
Secondary processing of the expression of pleasurable emotion	Secondary processing of emotional communication: sending of unpleasurable emotional signals; reception of both pleasant and uncomfortable feelings
	Reading body language
Facts	Events
Abstract processing	Concrete processing
Knowledge	Emotional significance of knowledge

Each hemisphere is divided into lobes. The lobes have distinct functions. As we watch the growing brain develop, these lobes will be discussed. The development of each region has its own timetable. With the proper stimulation, the lobes mature to create a unique brain. Figure 1.5 shows the brain's lobes, which include the following:

Occipital lobe. This lobe is responsible for vision. It is usually fully developed by age six.

Parietal lobe. It plays a part in the reception of sensory information. Also, the parietal lobe becomes active when problem solving and some calculations are attempted.

Brain Briefing

Touch activates many areas of the brain. Premature babies who were not touched and caressed did not develop as well or as fast as those who were (Rodriguez, 2007).

Temporal lobe. This lobe is responsible for hearing, some speech, and some memories.

Frontal lobe. This is the area responsible for controlling emotions, working memory, decision making, future planning, verbal expression, and voluntary movement. The frontal lobe can be further divided. We often refer to the area behind the forehead, which is called the prefrontal cortex. It is here that emotion is modulated, feelings are managed, and attention is focused (Sunderland, 2006).

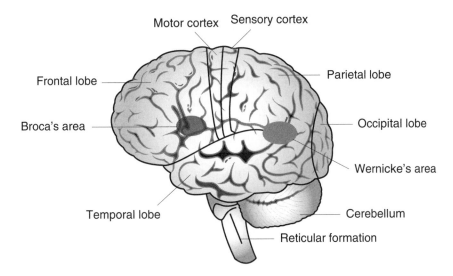

Figure 1.5   Lobes of the Brain

Also in Figure 1.5 you can see two important areas concerned with language and reading. **Broca's area** in the frontal lobe is responsible for expressive language. It puts words together syntactically and grammatically. **Wernicke's area**, in the parietal-temporal lobe, is responsible for receptive language. It stores the mental dictionary with the words and definitions you know. As these areas develop, language and reading skills will increase with proper stimuli.

Finally, notice the **reticular formation** in the brain stem. This structure helps with focus and attention. Its development is related to alertness. This structure helps us filter out some of the incoming information and attend to what we think is important.

> **Brain Briefing**
>
> According to neurologist Judy Willis (2006), it is the reticular formation that is changed by the fast paced media interactions and sensory stimulation that bombard our students. If you feel like you have to entertain your students to keep their attention, it may be due to the rapid pace at which they have to decide what to attend to.

BRAIN CHEMICALS

Early brain development includes the formation and release of chemicals in the brain. These **neurotransmitters** carry messages between neurons. They are released into the space between the sending axon and the receiving dendrites. This space is called a **synapse**, which is a communication point between two neurons (Figure 1.3). In the time between two months of gestation and two years after birth, about 15,000 synapses will form for every neuron in the cortex. The production of synapses as well as the pruning, or cutting back, of synapses is a large part of brain growth and development (Eliot, 1999). As synapses form, they provide more connecting points for dendrites and encourage the growth of **dendritic spines**, small nubs that are able to receive information. The growth of these spines is another indication of brain development. The spine is one half of the synapse, and the axon terminal is the other half. When the spine grows, a synapse is created. If the spine is pruned away, the synapse no longer exists.

The production and release of the following neurotransmitters will cause changes in the brain that will indicate growth and development:

Acetylcholine. Helps with frontal lobe functions and in formation of long-term memories.

Dopamine. Assists in focus, attention, and goal setting.

Norepinephrine. Responds to novelty and aids in memory formation.

Serotonin. Helps control impulsivity, calms the brain, aids in reflective behaviors.

ELECTROENCEPHALOGRAMS

EEGs, as electroencephalograms are called, are used to measure the electrical activity in the brain. We have looked at several chemicals that carry messages from one neuron to another, but the message that is transmitted within the neuron is electrical. For this reason, scientists have been able to monitor the brain's electrical activity and determine where and when this activity is strongest. This is another way to establish brain growth.

> **Brain Briefing**
>
> Human contact and touch promotes a sense of security and encourages healthy brain development. Neural networks grow out of our sensory experiences and begin forming the patterns for learning (Hannaford, 2005).

WINDOWS OF OPPORTUNITY

There are certain time periods when the brain appears to be very receptive to certain types of learning. These periods are called "windows of opportunity," the ideal time to provide the input that these active brain areas require. Simply put, these time periods will involve any or all of the following components:

1. Dendritic growth in a specific area: more receivers of information

2. Synaptic density in a specific area: more space for connections between neurons

3. Myelination of a specific area: faster and easier transmission of messages

4. Increase in brain wave activity

Although these windows do not slam shut, learning is much easier for the brain during these periods. Two windows are considered critical for normal development. Those windows are for vision and speech. If a baby is born with a cataract and it is not removed within the first several weeks of life, normal vision will not develop. That is not to say the child will not be able to see. It does indicate, at least, less than perfect vision. By the age of 12 a child will lose the ability to speak certain phonemes, so this is also a critical window, but one can see that with so many years allowed for development, this window closes slowly (Sousa, 2006).

> **Brain Briefing**
>
> IQ is not fixed at birth. Gone are the days of intelligence tests being able to predict the future for any child. Experience changes the brain (Healy, 2004).

John Bruer, in his landmark book *The Myth of the First Three Years* (2002), helped translate the research on these windows, which are sometimes called critical or sensitive periods. He assured readers that it was unnecessary to panic about these time periods.

Experience Dependent and Experience Expectant

Both neuroscientists and child development experts agree that there are two types of learning that occur (Berk, 2006; Bruer, 2001; Greenough, Black, & Wallace, 1987).

Experience-expectant learning relies on the assumption that circumstances will be present for learning to take place. Neural networks in the brain are expecting to form from specific stimuli that will be present. For instance, vision will develop as the eye is exposed to light and objects. It is expected that this will occur. Disruption of expectant sensory experience at the time the neurons are organizing and growing to meet that experience can cause irreversible damage (Kagan & Herschkowitz, 2004), but not all consequences are permanent. Vision develops slowly in infants, as you can see in Figure 1.6. This figure shows how well an infant can see, at varying ages, from a distance of 12 inches (approximately the distance from a caregiver's face when he or she is cradling a baby).

Newborn at 12 inches

Eight Weeks at 12 inches

Three Months at 12 inches

Six Months at 12 inches

Figure 1.6   This Shows How Well an Infant Can See From a 12-inch Distance

Experience-dependent learning occurs when the brain is exposed to certain types of experiences from the uniqueness of its environment. Neuroscientists often refer to the brain's "plasticity"— its ability to change from experience or from lack thereof. Children who hear the phonemes of their language will learn to repeat them. Those who experience chronic stress may have brains in which development is negatively affected. It is experience-dependent learning that is provided by the home, school, and other environments.

The sensitive periods with their approximate ages of optimal networking and consolidation are shown in Figure 1.7

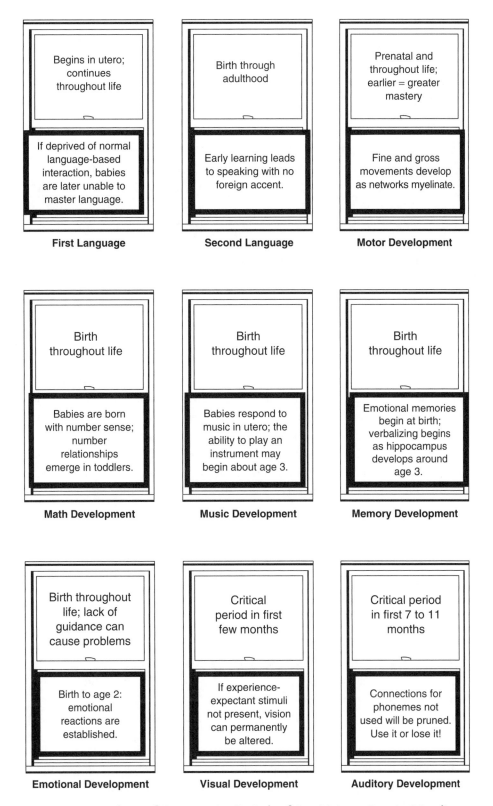

Figure 1.7   Windows of Opportunity: Periods of Sensitivity to Certain Stimuli
(Most windows never completely close)

First Language

There is every reason to believe that there are some critical periods for learning one's primary language. From several case studies, it appears likely that sometime between the ages of 6½ and 13, the brain's ability to learn a native language is changed (Bruer, 2002).

Brain Briefing

There is a famous case of a child called Genie who was kept isolated for 13 years. There was almost no verbal communication, and when she was finally found and released, she had no language skills. As she was properly cared for, she began to learn. Her language skills remained low as she spoke more like a two year old in very short sentences. Brain scans showed little activity in her left hemisphere (Sleeper, 2007).

Other children who suffered similar experiences were found much younger, around the age of six, and learned language quite well (Linden, 2007).

Second Language Learning

As many neuroscientists are studying the brain and learning, some conclusions have been made about the acquisition of a second language. Contrary to some beliefs that students are not ready to learn a second language until they are older, current research suggests that early exposure to a new language appears to be a better time for the brain to assimilate new accents, new vocabularies, and new grammar. Indeed, the brain can take its native language and use what it knows based on similarities and differences to make this learning easier. Yet, it appears that sometime in the second decade of life, it becomes more difficult to acquire such nuances as the appropriate accent (Bruer, 2002; Sousa, 2006).

Brain Briefing

Children learn their first language through sound, just as baby birds learn to sing by listening to adult birds. The auditory cortex, in the temporal lobe, must receive feedback by listening to others and listening to your own speech. This is also true of second language learning. The more one hears the new language, the better one learns it. Reading and writing the language are not as effective (Rodriguez, 2007).

In my own personal experience with this phenomenon, I taught several children in a family who came from France. The seventh grade twins, who had arrived in America at the age of six, had just the slightest accent on merely a few words. Their younger siblings had no accent whatsoever, but their mom and dad were difficult to understand, as their English was laced with their French accent.

Brain Briefing

In one famous study of Japanese children, it was found that at seven months they could hear the difference between the r and l sounds in English. At ten months, however, their auditory cortex had lost the ability to discriminate between the sounds (Begley, 2007).

Motor Development

Movement begins in the womb. When Amy was pregnant with Jack, she periodically declared he was doing jumping jacks. (Little did I know that this was a play on words; they didn't reveal his name until his birth.) Motor development continues throughout the early years, and actually as adults we can learn new motor skills. If we are to become experts or professionals at a certain skill, the earlier we begin to learn and practice, the better our chances will be at excelling (Sprenger, 2007). My son, Josh, learned this lesson the hard way. Although he was an avid tennis player during the summers of his elementary and middle school years, we couldn't afford to join a tennis club for him to play year round to keep up and hone his skills. When he tried out for the tennis team in high school, he soon discovered that all of the players who made the team had indeed been playing year round.

Memory Development

Emotional memories may be stored from birth, but since the hippocampus is not developed until around the age of three or four, the articulation of such memories is unlikely. Once the hippocampus begins to be involved in memory formation, long-term memory increases. It is at this time that children can tell us stories about their experiences in some detail and after some lengthy periods of time. Memory development continues throughout life if we take care of our brains and practice or rehearse some of the information we want to remember.

Music

There are certainly some mixed reports about the brain and music. It appears from several studies that the brain's response to music involves some of the same neurons that are utilized in math and other problem-solving endeavors (Dodge & Heroman, 1999).

Math

Several studies indicate that infants have some numeric sense. In one recent study involving well-known neuroscientist Michael Posner, it was confirmed that infants as young as six months old can detect errors in mathematics (Berger, Tzur, & Posner, 2006). Recent work at Duke University (Jordan & Brannon, 2006) concludes that babies have an innate number sense as early as seven months.

Emotion

At birth there are several emotional systems ready for survival. According to Sunderland (2006), rage, fear, and separation distress systems form. For this reason, responsive parenting and attachment to a primary caregiver are essential to controlling these systems and allowing the child the opportunity to learn how to calm him- or herself. Diamond and Hopson (1998) say that in the first 24 months, personality, temperament, and emotional reactions are established. Since the emotional system develops faster than the prefrontal lobe that helps control those emotions, it is necessary that someone else's frontal lobe help out.

Emotional development continues throughout childhood and possibly throughout our lives. Emotional intelligence as described by Goleman (1995, 1998; Goleman, Boyzatis, & McKee, 2002) includes the ability to recognize one's emotions, handle those emotions, recognize others' emotions, and handle relationships. These characteristics can begin to be modeled from infancy.

THINKING ABOUT BRAIN GROWTH

As we watch the brain develop in the following chapters, be aware of the following indicators of growth:

1. Synaptic density: More synapses are formed as neurons connect.

2. Myelination: Axons become coated with myelin sheaths.

3. Dendritic growth: New fibers form that receive information.

4. A spurt in production of certain neurotransmitters indicates activity in that area.

5. Increases in glucose consumption signify higher energy levels in the affected structures.

The connection from brain to behavior will depend on the areas that are showing growth. For instance, dendritic growth in the part of the corpus callosum that connects the hemispheres at the frontal lobe might indicate better working memory, higher-level thinking, or perhaps better impulse control.

Figure 2.1 Jack at One Year

Building the Brain Through Age Two

Jack is having his first birthday (Figure 2.1). It has been an exciting time for all of us. I have had the wonderful opportunity to spend several days per month in the company of this dendrite-growing, synapse-strengthening, myelinating mass of brain power. I have watched his vision improve and his motor skills emerge, and I witnessed his first steps (Figure 2.2)!

Figure 2.2   See Jack Run!

The sounds become more and more intelligible as he walks up to my son and utters, "Da, da, da . . ." In a few months he will deliberately connect his words with his actions, he will point to body parts, and he will understand our commands and requests.

Jack will throw tantrums when he can't do what he wishes. He will also become upset because he cannot tell us what he wants. Pointing will help him somewhat, but he will have much to say in his own little language that we will not understand.

> ### Brain Briefing
>
> A one-year-old has twice as many connections in his brain as his mother (Begley, 2007). For another year or two, a child's neurons continue connecting until each neuron has an average of 15,000 synaptic links.

Some of the little girls that he is with for playdates will be far ahead of Jack in language. Girls develop language skills before boys in many cases. According to Gurian (2007), the boy brain's ability to read and write is about one and one-half years behind the girl brain's ability.

Jack is learning baby sign language. He knows how to sign when he wants to eat, when he wants more, and when he is all done. Baby sign language has become popular, as research suggests that babies who sign have improved language skills and higher IQs (Goodwyn, Acredolo, & Brown, 2000). It is also known that the same areas used for speech (Broca's area and Wernicke's area) are also used for sign language.

Let's take a look at how Jack progressed from a sleeping, crying, nursing creature to a purposeful mover and conversationalist as well as how he will progress over the next two years.

BRAIN DEVELOPMENT

1. A newborn produces an immediate grasp reflex when a finger is placed in his or her palm. At three months, the reflex is gone due to synaptic connections from the cortex to the brain stem (Kagan & Herschkowitz, 2005).

2. By eight months there is a notable increase in activity in the frontal lobes, indicating higher cognitive functioning (Bergen & Coscia, 2001).

3. The limbic system matures between 6 and 18 months, when emotions can be felt and realized (Bergen & Coscia, 2001).

4. Vision is poor in a newborn, but during the first six months neurons grow and make connections in the occipital lobe and vision improves greatly (Eliot, 2006).

5. Directly after birth the cerebral cortex begins to myelinate. All areas have begun the process by the end of the first year. It all begins in the sensory areas and then the motor areas. The brain develops from back to front (Eliot, 2006).

6. Throughout the first three years of life, the brain continues to grow dendrites, myelinate, and create synapses. Some of this is genetically programmed; the rest is experience dependent. What happens to a baby in those first three years shapes the brain. First there is an overabundance of connections. Then there is a competition of sorts. The connections that are used remain, while the unused ones are pruned away (Gopnik, Meltzoff, & Kuhl, 1999).

Brain Briefing

Language is how we communicate with the world. Children understand their world through their experiences, many of which rely on speech and language. Language is learned quickly and begins as crying, cooing, and babbling that then progress to words and sentences. According to Sleeper (2007), most children go through the same steps but at their own pace.

LANGUAGE AND READING DEVELOPMENT

Prior to birth, babies are listening to language. They hear Mom's voice and will recognize it when they are born. The first step to reading is listening to the language. Babies try to put sounds together at about eight months. By that time, there should have been a lot of conversation between baby and others. Books should have been read on a daily basis. All of these things do make a difference!

- Language begins with some vocalization, coos, and babbles.

- Babies say single words, mimic sounds, and understand many words by the end of the 12th month.

- Between the ages of one and two, they begin using one-word sentences.

- Toward the middle to end of the second year, they combine words.

- Two-year-olds can say their own names and have a vocabulary of about 270 words.

- Between two and four, children start to understand speech (Herschkowitz & Herschkowitz, 2002).

- Language development is dependent on experience. Infants must hear the phonemes of their language if they are to create connections for those sounds before the synapses are pruned away.

- Books must be present in the home and read to the infant and toddler in order for them to develop their vocabularies, have background knowledge, and develop an appreciation for the sounds of the words.

During those first few years, it is important to talk to the baby. Explain exactly what you are doing and why. We start off with "parentese" (stretching out syllables and sounds in a singsong fashion) with infants. As they get older, spend some time talking with them in an almost normal tone using expression and explanations. This increases their vocabularies.

> ### Brain Briefing
>
> According to researcher Paula Tallal (2007), "parentese," the baby talk we use with infants, is what slows down and emphasizes the phonemes that will be part of the child's world. In this way, the sounds can be distinctly heard and connections for those sounds are made in the brain.

Children develop language and communication skills through social interaction. Face-to-face dialogue about what is going on in their world is important. Television does not provide the necessary interaction. The American Pediatric Association suggests no television for children under the age of two:

Pediatricians should urge parents to avoid television viewing for children under the age of 2 years. Although certain television programs may be promoted to this age group, research on early brain development shows that babies and toddlers have a critical need for direct interactions with parents and other significant caregivers (e.g., child care providers) for healthy brain growth and the development of appropriate social, emotional, and cognitive skills. Therefore, exposing such young children to television programs should be discouraged. (Public Broadcasting System, 2002–2007)

PHYSICAL AND MOTOR DEVELOPMENT

The number of physical changes between birth and the end of the second year is incredible. Children seem to learn motor skills overnight. From seemingly total helplessness to running around like a whirling dervish—it appears to happen in a blink of an eye. Movement builds the brain. Dendrites will grow and strengthen as the child practices lifelong skills through physical play.

Brain Briefing

Movement begins in utero and continues throughout life. Movement develops the vestibular system, which allows for balance. It builds the cerebellum, which is involved in both movement and cognitive activities. One could look at movement as the opportunity for the cerebellum to practice making connections that it will need for higher level thinking. According to Hannaford (2005), real learning does not take place without movement.

Gross Motor Skills

Remember, these ages are approximate!

- Lifts head (two months)
- Rolls over (three to five months; with the new rule about babies sleeping on their backs and given minimal "tummy time," rolling over is sometimes achieved a bit later)
- Sits without support (six months)
- Walks holding on to furniture or hand (nine months)
- Stands on his own for a number of seconds (10 months)
- Stands alone (11 months)
- Walks alone (12 months)
- Walks backwards (14 months)

- Walks steps (17 months)

- Kicks a ball forward (18 months)

- Jumps (24 months)

- Climbs up and down stairs, runs, climbs on and off furniture (two years)

Fine Motor Skills

- Grasping a rattle begins at three or four months.

- Reaching begins around four or five months.

- The thumb-finger grasp may begin around seven months and be followed in a few months by putting blocks into a cup.

- Scribbling starts around one year.

- Tower building begins shortly after the first birthday, and imitating a vertical line comes between two and three (Herschkowitz & Herschkowitz, 2002).

SOCIAL AND EMOTIONAL DEVELOPMENT

By six months babies are learning about their feelings and how to manage them—mostly from Mom and Dad. When babies are picked up and soothed, for example, they are being taught how to soothe themselves and how to handle distress.

- At seven months they are aware of strangers.

- Between 7 and 13 months, they play pat-a-cake or other clapping games.

- At 15 months, they are very loving and affectionate.

- By 18 months a toddler is learning emotional intelligence skills from people other than Mom and Dad. Age-appropriate books, for example, can enhance the children's understanding of their feelings, so read stories that deal with emotions.

- At two years, they play alongside others but not with them. They hold on to toys if someone else wants them.

- Between ages two and three, they begin to play with others.

COGNITIVE DEVELOPMENT

Cognitive development involves problem solving, concentration, memory, symbolic thought, and inquisitiveness. All children learn differently, and their approach to learning may vary (Altmann, 2006).

- Between six and nine months, children can detect simple arithmetic errors (Berger, Tzur, & Posner, 2006).

- By seven months of age, infants connect numerical representations across different sensory modalities (Jordan & Brannon, 2006).

- Between ages one and two, toddlers try a variety of physical strategies to reach simple goals. For example, Jack gets his walker wagon stuck as he pushes it into the couch. He used to just whine until we helped him, but now he tries to figure out how to move it so he can continue his journey (Figure 2.3).

Figure 2.3   Jack and His Walker Wagon

- At about 12 months, infants use gestures and simple language to get help when "stuck." Jack raises his arms toward me and says, "Up up!" when trying to get over the gate to the cats.

- At 15 months, toddlers can make some animal sounds; they know about five words, including names. They know what a dog or a cat is.

- At 18 months, they can imitate a drawing stroke and may follow simple commands.

- At 2 years, a toddler's vocabulary is increasing quickly. They point to objects and name them, and they obey complicated orders.

- They recognize and name one color between the ages of 2½ and 3¾.

- By 3, they are asking questions constantly. They build structures that are somewhat complicated, remember the past, and can copy a circle.

DEVELOPMENTALLY APPROPRIATE ACTIVITIES FROM BIRTH THROUGH AGE TWO

Reading and Language Development

- Talk, talk, talk.

- Read, read, read! Read to the child every day. Sit the child on your lap and read into his or her ear. In this way they see the appropriate way to hold and read a book.

> ### Brain Briefing
>
> Holding a book correctly and reading to the child allows him or her to see that you are reading from left to right. The connections taking place in your brain will actually begin to take place in the child's brain (Restak, 2001). This is a great beginning to reading. In addition, you are modeling enthusiasm for reading, fluency, and intonation.

- Sing, sing, sing!

- The chewing stage is important for reading. Give children books that won't be damaged by chewing. Cloth books and board books work well. Children learn about their world through their senses. Chewing a book is the child's first interaction with it. Eventually, there will be interest in the pictures and the words. At 10 months, Jack suddenly loved his books and would spend time going through each one of them (Figure 2.4).

Figure 2.4 At 10 Months, Jack Loved His Books

- When you talk to babies, look directly at them, and pause for responses. Consider any sound they make to be dialogue. Give them a turn to speak. In this way they learn how conversation is give and take.

- Read nursery rhymes or rhyming stories and books. When children rhyme, it means they understand some important points about language. It is the beginning of phonemic awareness, the first step toward reading.

Brain Briefing

Early knowledge of nursery rhymes is specifically related to strong word processing skills and to future reading ability (Maclean, Bryant, & Bradley, 1987). Since the brain is drawn to rhythm and rhyme, this type of reading offers an opportunity for the one-year-old to appreciate the sounds and partake in a fun activity. Distinguishing between sounds with a loving caregiver enhances this experience and helps to create a love of learning.

- Elaborate. If the child comes to you with a truck or rock or anything else, talk about the object. For instance, when my daughter Marnie was little, she brought a chameleon into the house. I had to keep myself from freaking out, since lizards were not my favorites. My first inclination was to say, "Marnie, take that back outside!" But I also knew that I would be missing a teachable moment. So I began by asking her what she had and continued the conversation as we learned from each other and the encyclopedia about the creature. (Then I made her take it outside!)

Brain Briefing

According to Hart and Risley (1995), the limited vocabulary of children of lower socioeconomic status comes from the lack of elaboration during conversations with parents or caregivers. Their research states that children from professional families hear about 11 million words per year. Middle class children hear about 6 million words. Welfare children hear about 3 million. Children that hear more words before age three will experience improved student achievement later in school.

Physical and Motor Development

One-year-olds may be walking, although some are not quite ready yet. They will be climbing, crawling, reaching (those little arms can stretch like rubber bands when they see something they want), opening and closing (drawers, cabinets, boxes, cell phones, etc.), pushing walkers, pulling toys, and giving everyone exercise as they try to keep up! Closer to the two-year mark, toddlers will be climbing steps, running, kicking balls (and other things!) as well as carrying several items while moving. As the three-year mark approaches, there will be more control and less falling, and pedaling a tricycle will be part of the program.

These activities will help develop gross motor skills:

- Provide cushions to climb on.

- Create small obstacle courses in the living room.

- Climb stairs behind them as they crawl up.

- Use a large playground ball and roll the ball to the child. Ask the child to roll it back.

- Play Red Light–Green Light. One person stands at the front and gives instructions. Red light means stop. Green light means go, and they can move around as much as they'd like. Yellow light means move slowly.

- Freeze dance: Play music while everyone dances. Stop the music, and dancers must freeze in position.

- Play Follow the Leader. Choose a leader, and everyone does whatever the leader does. Often they are in line behind the leader.

- Jumping is possible for children between the ages of two and three. You might hold the child's hand at first, or hop off of a low step.

- Encourage rolling over, sitting up, creeping, climbing, pulling up, standing, and walking.

- Encourage jumping, throwing, hopping, and dancing.

- Put a small tent up in the classroom. Put books and small toys inside. Let the children crawl around inside. It's a great place to read.

- Keep the box that your new refrigerator (or HD TV) comes in. Cut out some holes and make a fort for the children.

- Get a sandbox, small shovels, and buckets. Pretend you are digging for gold.

- Go to the playground or to the park and swing. Go down the slide together. Climb on the monkey bars.

These activities will help develop fine motor skills:

- Provide blocks, and model how to build a tower.

- Pull out the plastic containers for food storage. Show the child how to nest them inside each other.

- Turn pages in a book (Figure 2.5).

Figure 2.5   Jack Uses His New Fine Motor Skills to Point to a Picture in a Book

- Fill up a sink, push a chair in front of it, and let toddlers play with plastic cups. This will keep them busy, provide fine motor practice, and teach physics as well.

- Draw.

- Paint.

- Play with snap beads or Legos.

- Practice zipping.

Cognitive Development

Learning through trial and error is an important way to make strong connections in the brain. Opportunities to try, fail, and try again should be prevalent beginning before the second birthday and continuing throughout life. Obstacles are part of problem solving and learning. Be sure not to overindulge a child by solving problems for them; this denies them the opportunity to create the networks in their brains that will be useful as other challenges loom (Shaefer & DiGeronimo, 2000).

- Incorporate numbers and counting into everything you do.

- Develop memory by reminding the child of what happened in the past.

- Play matching games for memory, where the child has to match objects that go together.

- Play games like peekaboo and pat-a-cake to increase memory skills.

Brain Briefing

Peekaboo is an important game that research suggests can be played with four-month-olds. The social implications are strong as children interact with their caregivers. A reward system is also involved in this simple game. The important neurotransmitter dopamine is released in the brain as the child feels good about playing and discovering what is hidden. This chemical will also be involved in attention and focus, which are exactly what are used in peekaboo (Sunderland, 2006).

- Find patterns in the world. There are patterns in songs, in wildlife, in speech, and in puzzles.

- Have puzzles with large pieces on hand after the chewing stage ends!

Brain Briefing

It is now thought that the terrible twos begin at age one and don't end until age four. We have to give these infants and toddlers the benefit of the doubt, as most of them are delightful. Those that are born with a sensitive temperament may not get the same love and attention as happy babies. When parents don't feel that they can make their child happy, sometimes they give up and tend to the children who respond positively to them (Perry & Szalavitz, 2007).

Figure 3.1   The Irresistible Adam

The Three-Year-Old Brain

Adam (Figure 3.1) has a talent for altering the truth. He lies. But not well. He will insist that he did not drink the soda from the empty glass in front of him. Although he exaggerates and makes up information that he shares as true, he is irresistible to his mom and dad because Adam is deeply in love with them. He will spontaneously show his affections.

Adam's preschool teacher is pleased with his progress. He is beginning to interact with others in his class. Like most three-year-olds, Adam likes routine at school. His teacher uses many procedures and rituals that the children respond to.

When given directions at home or school, Adam is now able to follow them as long as they contain no more than two or three parts: "Go upstairs, get your pajamas on, and brush your teeth." Adam will be able to do this; however, he may hop up the steps if he is not running.

Candyland is one of Adam's favorite board games. He can sit and play with his family for a short period of time. Sometimes Adam picks up the game pieces and announces what color they are. Sometimes he simply throws them! While playing, Adam may run around the table or kick his brother.

Angie, his mother, is concerned that Adam my have Attention Deficit Hyperactivity Disorder. It is really too early to make that diagnosis (Amen, 2006).

Figure 3.2   Adam and Friend

Three-year-olds are a handful, yet they are loving and fun loving (Figure 3.2). At this age children have begun to tell stories. Their memories are just developing, yet they may include interesting details in their storytelling (Eliot, 1999).

Adam greets guests at the door with his mom. As soon as he realizes the visitor is okay, he begins talking about anything—his dog, or another playmate, or anything he currently finds favorable.

Stimulating the brain growth of three-year-olds is crucial. As physical growth slows down somewhat, emotional and cognitive growth show great increases (Shevlov, 2004). Adam loves the soothing music his teacher plays. It calms him when he needs some relaxing time. Music and musical instruments are very appealing to this three-year-old. At preschool, toy pianos and drums are some of the instruments provided.

BRAIN DEVELOPMENT

Three-year-olds have enormous changes occurring in their brains. They are ready for a more focused, reflective view of life as the brain prunes away unnecessary connections as determined by the experiences of the next five years. As the prefrontal cortex develops, it can assist the temporal lobe, which helps the three-year-old expand his or her memory and speak more clearly (Siegel, 1999).

> **Brain Briefing**
>
> By the age of three, the child's brain is two and one-half times more active than the adult brain. One could look at this information as proof that this is a prime time for learning (Linden, 2007). At three years old, a child's brain is about 90 percent of its adult size.

1. Between the ages of two and three years, connections between the hippocampus, neocortex, and limbic system become stronger (Hershkowitz & Hershkowitz, 2006). This would imply that the brain is beginning to be able to store long-term semantic memories. Since the limbic system includes the amygdala, our primitive structure for emotions, emotional learning can encourage a great deal of factual and conceptual learning.

2. As the child approaches the age of three, blood flow becomes greater in the left hemisphere (Hershkowitz & Hershkowitz, 2006). A language "explosion" occurs around the age of three. This greater blood flow in the hemisphere associated with the production and understanding of language may be a sign of great strides in speech and language development.

3. The corpus callosum connects the frontal lobes (Kagan & Hershkowitz, 2005). As the two hemispheres strengthen their connections in the executive area of the brain, three-year-olds may develop higher-level thinking skills, increased language skills, and better emotional skills.

4. Language dominance switches from the right hemisphere to the left. During the first three years of life, blood flow is heavier in the right hemisphere. During these years children are engaged in understanding and interpreting messages. At three, they will begin to concentrate on communicating and need more glucose in the left hemisphere (Healy, 2004).

5. This age also sees increased synaptic density in the connections between Broca's and Wernicke's areas, which deal with language and reading (Sousa, 2006). Since blood flow is greater in the left hemisphere, these language structures are receiving the energy they need to create and increase connectivity. As this occurs, speech and vocabulary increase.

6. Episodic memory begins to emerge (Siegel, 1999). This memory system, which is associated with events and locations, allows three-year-olds to make sense of occurrences and makes them better able to tell and retell stories and events in their lives.

7. The cerebellum is continuing myelination and growth to make stronger connections between the frontal and parietal lobes. Since birth, these areas have been connecting, and this process will continue throughout the preschool period. Gains in visual-motor coordination will be seen. These connections will help children physically and cognitively (Berk, 2006).

These changes are summarized in Figure 3.3.

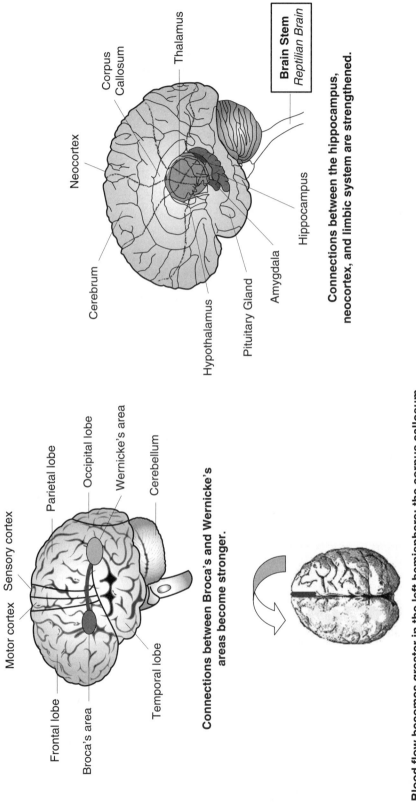

Figure 3.3 Changes in a Three-Year-Old's Brain

> **Brain Briefing**
>
> Keep in mind that brains develop according to their own timetables. Nature and nurture work together to create the person that each three-year-old will be! Some will develop faster than others (Eliot, 1999).

LANGUAGE AND READING DEVELOPMENT

Fox (2001) states that children need to have had about 1000 stories read to them before they will be able to read. One can imagine the differences between children who come from homes with a high level of literacy and those who come from homes where books are not available. I always tell the teachers I train that if they read a child the first book he or she has ever heard, they must keep in mind, "Only 999 books to go!" At least, there is a goal.

Three-year-olds love to talk. Those who have had little dialogue at home may need some prompts, but most quickly want to join in conversations. The more opportunity they have, the more their speech improves along with their vocabulary and sentence structure. Ask a three-year-old a question, and be prepared to hear a story.

Three-year-olds

- speak in sentences of five or six words.
- have speech that is clearly understood.
- like to tell stories.
- know some basic grammar.
- can identify most common objects.
- offer related responses to questions (Healy, 2004).
- change topics quickly when speaking (Healy, 2004).
- take turns talking.
- can use language for different purposes (asking, telling, etc.).

> **Brain Briefing**
>
> The concepts of who, what, and where are understood between the ages of three and four. All types of grammatical constructions are used by three-year-olds, but they will not perfect their construction until they reach age four or five (Sleeper, 2007).

PHYSICAL AND MOTOR DEVELOPMENT

Although most brain development points to more cognitive and emotional growth, three-year-olds continue their motor development and require practice to strengthen their physical abilities.

Three-year-olds

- hop, kick, run, and climb.
- balance on one foot.
- have improving eye-hand coordination.
- can pedal a tricycle.
- can bend over and keep their balance.

Three-year-olds' fine motor skills include

- turning pages one at a time.
- stacking up to six blocks.
- holding a pencil correctly.
- screwing and unscrewing lids.
- playing the piano (not necessarily harmoniously)!

SOCIAL AND EMOTIONAL DEVELOPMENT

This is an important time to be particularly encouraging and supportive. Three-year-olds need guidelines and rules as they learn to interact with others. Major changes in routine can be quite upsetting to these little people (Brookes, 2006).

Three-year-olds

- pretend.
- may have an imaginary friend.
- begin to play board games.
- separate from parents easily.
- are in love with Mom and Dad and pretend to be them.
- may become terrible liars.
- like routine.
- move back and forth from fantasy to reality.

Brain Briefing

It is important to talk with three-year-olds about both positive and negative emotions. Although there is a tendency to talk about positive emotions as they occur, sometimes negative emotions are not discussed until another time, since they are not "fun" to talk about. Regulating negative emotions is more difficult for children, so these feelings need to be talked about. Research suggests that when adults talk to children about negative emotions, they are more likely to learn to control them (Hirsh-Pasek & Golinkoff, 2003).

COGNITIVE DEVELOPMENT

As speech centers mature and connections between lobes continue to grow stronger, three-year-olds can share what they know and learn many new things.
Three-year-olds

- know some colors and can sort objects by color and shape.

- can follow procedures with up to three steps.

- recognize similarities and differences.
  - o This is such an important development. Helping students to identify similarities and differences is the number-one way to raise student achievement, according to scientifically based research (Marzano, Pickering, & Pollack, 2001). This is certainly an area that needs to be developed throughout the school years.

- remember stories.

- pretend.

- understand numbers and counting.

- complete puzzles with three or four pieces.

- may begin to use memory strategies (Eliot, 1999).

DEVELOPMENTALLY APPROPRIATE ACTIVITIES FOR THREE-YEAR-OLD BRAINS

Neuroscientists encourage the use of multimodal experiences for the young brain, and indeed, for all brains (Eide & Eide, 2006; Herschkowitz & Herschkowitz, 2006; Peterson, 2001). Keep in mind that child care centers that provide sensory stimulation, such as water tables, sand tables, artwork with varying media (chalk, paints, crayons, markers, etc.) will offer three-year-olds the opportunity to develop different areas of their brains. The following strategies are categorized, but please keep in mind that many of these activities promote growth in several areas.

For Language and Reading Development

- Read to the children every day.

- Tell stories and ask children to retell them

- Use extended questions: After reading a story, ask higher-level or deeper questions rather than questions with single-word answers.
  - o Lower level: What was the boy's name?
  - o Higher level: How do you think the boy felt?

- Play rhyming games.

- Pronounce three words such as cat, hat, and man. Ask the children to identify the word that sounds different.

- Read nursery rhymes and play sound games with those rhymes.

○ Replace the first letters of words to show children how a sound can change the rhyme. For example,

From: Jack be nimble, Jack be quick. Jack jump over the candlestick!
To: Zack be nimble . . .
Or: Jack jump over the candlewick!

- Show the children three pictures of things, and ask them to identify the things whose names or words rhyme (Figure 3.4).

Figure 3.4 Which Two Rhyme?

- Point to an object in the room, and ask the children to say a word that rhymes with it.
  ○ Point to the clock, and ask them what they are wearing that rhymes with it (sock).
  ○ Point to a pen, and ask what farm animal rhymes with it (hen).

- Sing rhyming songs. "Down by the Bay" by Raffi is a good example.

Brain Briefing

The ability to hear rhymes and alliterations is vital to learning to read (Tallal, 2007). Focus on literature that deals playfully with speech sounds. Dr. Seuss books are always good for this, as are nursery rhymes.

For Physical and Motor Development

- Physical movement is very important. Skipping is reading readiness (Wesson, 2005). Provide incentive for this activity. Play skipping songs (such as "Skip to My Lou"), or read skipping books.

- Introduce students to museums and zoos. Investigate those that allow more hands-on experiences for children.

- Create simple obstacle courses in the classroom or on the playground. Give three-year-olds a chance to learn new physical skills.

- Freeze dance: Play music while everyone dances. Stop the music, and everyone must freeze in position.

- Play Red Light–Green Light. One person stands at the front and gives instructions. Red light means stop. Green light means go, and they can move around as much as they'd like. Yellow light means move slowly.
- A twist on Twister: Place different colors of construction paper on the ground. As you call out a color, children must touch the color with a hand or foot or even a knee. This is great fun, encourages color identification, and works on motor skills.

For Social and Emotional Development

- Provide a dress up area. Social and emotional intelligence can be learned and enhanced by role-playing real life situations. Shopper and grocery checker, waiter/waitress and diner, teacher and student, doctor and patient are all possible scenarios. Let students create their own.
- Encourage emotional intelligence.
  - At this age, emotional awareness is crucial to healthy learning. Ask students to identify their feelings. This may begin with games. Show students smiley faces showing distinct feelings (Figure 3.5). Ask them what they think this face is feeling. Allow them to make those same faces, look at each other, and in so doing begin to see what these feelings look like on a real face.

Figure 3.5   Emotional Intelligence Faces

- Encourage children to say good things about themselves.
  - Play the song "I Like Me" and ask children to sing and move to the music. Then go around the class and ask children to give one reason why they like themselves.
  - Read the book "I Like Me" by Nancy Carlson (1988), and follow the same procedure.

For Cognitive Development

- The Mad Hatter: An old coat rack is a great place for lots of interesting hats. Children can "become" whoever the hat represents—a chef, a sailor, or a police officer. Create an atmosphere where the students can role-play the different community members they may interact with.

> ### Brain Briefing
>
> Parents need to understand brain development. Help them become partners in the process of developing their children's brains. Encourage them to participate by giving their three-year-old opportunities at home. A three-year-old can set the table!

- Play memory games: Provide pairs of animal cards or cards with shapes, colors, or numbers. Turn them over and have children turn over two cards at a time to see if they match. Then continue this memory game as they find the matching pairs.

- Hold up geometric shapes and ask children to identify similarities and differences in them. If they can also identify the shapes, begin by asking them to do so.

  This is a _____. That's right, "square." This is a _____. That's right, "triangle." How are these different?

- Use counting songs and rhymes.

  One potato, two potato, Three potato, four. Five potato, six potato Seven potato, more.

- Or take the song "B-i-n-g-o" and add the children's names:

  There is a girl who comes to school,
  And Keisha is her name—o
  K-e-i-s-h-a, K-e-i-s-h-a, K-e-i-s-h-a,
  And Keisha is her name—o!

> ### Brain Briefing
>
> After age two or three, the process of pruning begins. Pruning is a loss of synapses. This is a positive change in the brain, as the connections that are used will remain, while those with little traffic are removed. Compare this process to paths in the woods. Those that are trod on often will remain free of weeds and other growth. The paths that are not used are soon lost in the overgrowth of plant life (Sprenger, 1999).

The cofounder of New Directions Institute for Infant Brain Development, Dr. Jill Stamm, reminds us of the importance of downtime for children. As we promote activities for youngsters to wire their brains for success, we must also allow them time to work on those connections (Stamm & Spencer, 2007). As adults, we give ourselves brain breaks to help refocus and refresh our minds. So should we do this with our young students.

Child Development Checklist: Three-Year-Olds

Name _____   Grade _____

Birth date _____   Chronological Age _____

LANGUAGE and READING DEVELOPMENT

____ Speaks in sentences of five or six words

____ Speech is clearly understood

____ Likes to tell stories

____ Knows some basic grammar

____ Can identify most common objects

____ Offers related response to questions

____ Changes topics quickly when speaking

____ Takes turns talking

____ Can use language for different purposes

Recommendations for increasing reading and language growth:

_____

_____

_____

PHYSICAL and MOTOR DEVELOPMENT

____ Hops   ____ Balances on one foot

____ Improving eye-hand coordination   ____ Climbs

____ Kicks   ____ Runs

____ Can pedal a tricycle   ____ Bends over and keeps balance

Fine motor skills

____ Turns pages one at a time

____ Stacks up to six blocks

____ Holds a pencil correctly

____ Screws and unscrews lids

____ Has the ability to play piano

Recommendations for increasing physical and motor growth:

_____

_____

_____

SOCIAL and EMOTIONAL GROWTH

___ Pretends	___ May have an imaginary friend
___ Begins to play board games	___ Separates from parents easily
___ Is in love with Mom and Dad	___ Becomes a terrible liar
___ Likes routine	___ Moves back and forth from fantasy to reality

Recommendations for increasing social and emotional growth:

_____

_____

_____

COGNITIVE GROWTH

___ Knows some colors

___ Can follow procedures up to three steps

___ Recognizes similarities and differences

___ Remembers stories

___ Pretends

___ Understands numbers and counting

___ Begins to use memory strategies

___ Puts puzzles consisting of two or three pieces together

Recommendations for increasing cognitive growth:

_____

_____

_____

Figure 4.1 Benjamin

The Four-Year-Old Brain

S ay hello to Benjamin! This four-year–old (Figure 4.1) is acting silly today. He often tells stories or jokes that he thinks are funny. Be prepared to cover your ears for several reasons: Ben is loud, Ben sometimes uses inappropriate language such as profanity, and he can get very angry and throw tantrums.

Tantrums are difficult for both Mom and Ben's preschool teachers. Current research tells us that this type of behavior is increasing rather than decreasing. The more television children watch, the more disruptive they are by the time they reach school age (Certain & Kahn, 2002).

On a brighter note, Ben is very curious and active. He likes to try all sorts of new adventures. Physically, he is very energetic and beginning to be quite agile. He can now throw, bounce, and catch a ball quite easily.

At preschool Ben is actively engaged. He enjoys other children and plays fairly well. Sharing is not a problem for Ben, but he often likes to boss others around. His teacher finds that Ben carries on elaborate conversations, and because he doesn't understand the concept of telling lies, sometimes his imagination runs away with him.

On occasion Benjamin is quite fearful and senses danger when there probably isn't any. It is helpful that his teacher has set up daily routines and rituals to lower his stress and help him feel safe. He can also become quite jealous of others and tends to brag about his own possessions.

Kyle is one of Ben's friends in the preschool classroom (Figure 4.2). Kyle has no siblings and is not used to Ben's bossiness, but they like to be together on the playground. Kyle has a dog, and Ben has offered to trade his older brother for Kyle's pet!

Figure 4.2   Kyle

Ben's teacher knows that pretending is important to her students. Props are provided so they can elaborate settings and situations. She also provides opportunities for the four-year-olds to tell stories to younger students at school.

BRAIN DEVELOPMENT

From late in the third year through the fourth year, the brain is changing and maturing. Counting, storytelling, and make-believe are all part of the early childhood experience. As the brain continues to develop, language improves, number sense continues, and curiosity accelerates.

1. Math areas begin to develop in the parietal lobe (Berk, 2006). Four-year-olds can do some counting, usually up to seven—and sometimes in the right order! Some basic understandings related to number are seen.

2. Myelination between the frontal lobes continues to accelerate (Kagan & Herschkowitz, 2005). As the frontal lobes continue to connect, this child will be able to make associations between the big picture and smaller details.

3. Myelination in the limbic area continues (Kagan & Herschkowitz, 2005). The four-year-old child is interacting with other children as well as adults. As the emotional area of the brain continues development, the child will have more stable and intimate relationships.

4. More dendritic growth occurs in Broca's area (Eliot, 1999). Since language abilities are continuing to grow, it makes sense that this important language and reading structure is making more connections. Sentences become more grammatically correct, and syntax improves.

5. Glucose utilization is twice that of adults (Chugani, 1999). This busy brain is taking in more of the world, as sensory information is introduced at a fast pace. In order to handle all of this input, the brain utilizes about 30 percent of the body's energy.

6. Pruning of the prefrontal cortex continues. All of the synapses that were formed in the first two or three years of life cannot remain. The brain certainly follows the rule of "Use it or lose it!" Those synapses that have not been used will be snipped away (Eliot, 2007).

7. Neurons that produce acetylcholine appear after the fourth birthday (Kagan & Herschkowitz, 2005). Remember that this neurotransmitter aids in long-term memory. By age four, the hippocampus is developed and is forming impersonal memories.

8. The cerebellum is continuing myelination and the frontal and parietal lobes are growing. Since birth these areas have been connecting, and they will continue to connect throughout the preschool period. Gains in visual-motor coordination will be seen. These connections will help children physically and cognitively (Berk, 2006). When they start school, children will be able to throw and catch a ball, print letters, and play games such as hopscotch.

These changes are summarized in Figure 4.3.

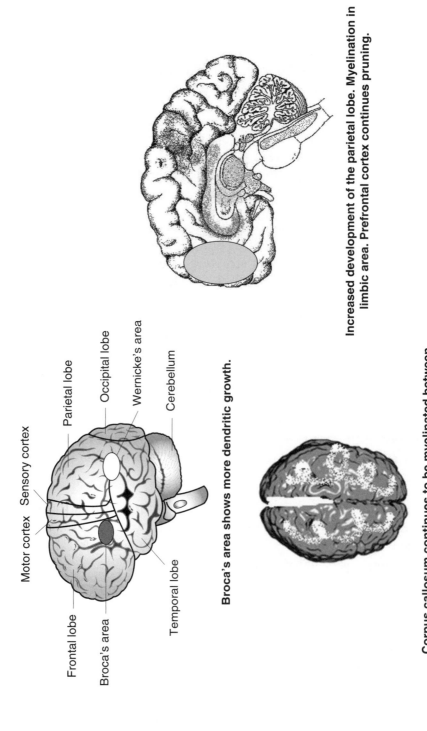

Frontal lobe

Broca's area

Motor cortex   Sensory cortex

Parietal lobe

Occipital lobe

Wernicke's area

Cerebellum

Temporal lobe

Broca's area shows more dendritic growth.

Increased development of the parietal lobe. Myelination in limbic area. Prefrontal cortex continues pruning.

Corpus callosum continues to be myelinated between frontal lobes; glucose utilization high.

Figure 4.3   Changes in a Four-Year-Old's Brain

48

> ### Brain Briefing
>
> Both personal and impersonal memories help children learn. Personal memories are sometimes called autobiographical or episodic memories. Impersonal memories are semantic memories, which deal more with factual information and concepts that are not related to our own lives. When teaching engages students on a personal level, many children have a better chance of storing information. For instance, taking information and putting it in story form offers students a setting and characters to remember and relate to (Eide & Eide, 2006; Sprenger, 1999).

LANGUAGE AND READING DEVELOPMENT

Four-year-olds talk even more than three-year-olds. It seems as though they never run out of things to share. Being read to is a treat. Reciprocal reading is enjoyable. You read to me, and I'll read to you! Although their "reading" is often telling the part of the story that is on their page rather than reading the words, it is certainly a step in the right direction! They may still like to read the same book again and again. Remember, the brain is strengthening the neural connections each time that story is read. Plus, at this tender age, brains focus on specific parts of the story and need repetition to become more familiar with the whole story.

Four-year-olds

- have an expanding vocabulary.
- will repeat curse words.
- use complete sentences.
- enjoy singing simple songs.
- think rhymes and nonsense words are fun.
- may add "ed" to words (both correctly and incorrectly) to form the past tense.
- adjust their language for their audience (speak baby talk to little ones; use a larger vocabulary for adults).
- can spell their names aloud.
- can identify uppercase letters.
- can print their own names.
- can put story cards in a sequence.

> ### Brain Briefing
>
> According to Jim Trelease, author of the best-selling *The Read Aloud Handbook* (2001), there are three books that contain all of the phonemes, blends, and diphthongs a child needs to hear. They are *Goodnight Moon*, *Make Way for Ducklings,* and *Charlotte's Web*.

Figure 4.4   Physical Ben

PHYSICAL AND MOTOR DEVELOPMENT

Motor skills of the four-year-old are great now that this child has the balance and coordination of an adult (Shelov, 2004) (Figure 4.4). Although physical skills are many, judgment is not as developed, and four-year-olds may let their bodies get ahead of themselves. Running when they should be walking is one example. Fine motor skills are also improving now. Encouraging arts and crafts will help the four-year-olds further develop these emerging abilities.

Four-year-olds

- climb.

- swing.

- turn somersaults.

- hop.

- may skip.

- can stand on one foot.

Brain Briefing

Just as crawling was important to activate both hemispheres and to activate the cerebellum, skipping is important to the reading process. Although skipping may not be learned during this important fourth year, opportunities to learn the skill should be offered (Hannaford, 2004; Wesson, 2005).

Four-year-olds' fine motor skills include

- tracing.
- building.
- drawing.
- writing (scribbling).
- finger painting.

SOCIAL AND EMOTIONAL DEVELOPMENT

Although still bossy, four-year-olds will begin to make friends. They can show sympathy and begin to understand others' feelings. As their sense of humor develops, four-year-olds laugh at funny incidents and sometimes overdo it by being boisterous and loud. At other times they may whisper secrets to others. Four-year-olds show more interest in children than adults (Herr & Larson, 2004).

Four-year-olds

- may have imaginary friends.
- may tattle or call others names.
- want to please.
- like to sing and dance.
- have active fantasy lives.
- may still lie.
- are influenced by their friends' behavior.
- base their friendships on shared activities.
- exclude children they don't like.

> ### Brain Briefing
>
> It is never too early to begin emotional coaching. As children play together, there are bound to be moments where emotions get high. Teaching four-year-olds how to handle those interactions and discussing their feelings can help them learn how to recognize their own and others' emotions and how to handle relationships (Goleman, 1995).

COGNITIVE DEVELOPMENT

Basic concepts begin to be appreciated. The four-year-old may understand that the day is divided into segments: morning, afternoon, and evening. Concepts of time such as weeks, days, hours, and minutes are beginning to be understood.

Four-year-olds

- learn by doing.
- can count from five to seven items.
- can compare sets of items.
- accurately name four or more colors.
- love being read to.
- like to label and classify the environment.
- can tell you their name, address, and phone number (near the end of the fourth year).
- may be able to copy their own names.
- draw people with basic large body parts (head, arms, legs, trunk).
- question many things (death, sex, etc.).

DEVELOPMENTALLY APPROPRIATE ACTIVITIES FOR FOUR-YEAR-OLD BRAINS

Continue to use the activities for three-year-olds and add these suggested activities and others. Again, these are categorized here, but most activities help in several developmental areas.

For Language and Reading Development

- Read to four-year-olds every day. Provide a book center with interesting and colorful picture books of different sizes and shapes.
- Provide a variety of reading materials, such as magazines, coupons, and cereal boxes.
- Read nursery rhymes and continue to play rhyming games.
- Encourage four-year-olds to tell stories to younger children.
- Give four-year-olds several pictures along with printed words that rhyme with the objects in the pictures. Have them match each picture to its rhyming word (Figure 4.5).

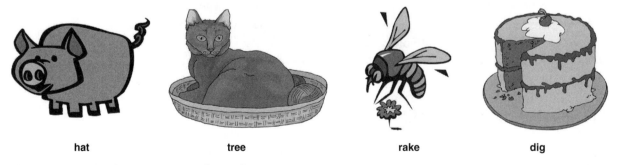

hat   tree   rake   dig

Figure 4.5   Matching-Pictures-With-Words

Brain Briefing

Four-year-olds should sing. When they are singing, they learn new vocabulary words. They learn rhythm to help them with prosody, the stress and intonation patterns of words and sentences. They learn rhyme to help them with phonemic awareness. Music has changing inflections, tones, and rhythms just like language (Schaefer & DiGeronimo, 2000).

For Physical and Motor Development

- Continue to play skipping games as you would for three-year-olds.

- Play games like Follow the Leader to encourage physical development. Let the students use their imaginations as they walk like different animals or "swim like a fish."

- Create obstacle courses, so four-year-olds can learn to maneuver their bodies.

- Play Simon Sez (I call it "Sprenger Sez" with my students) to reinforce listening skills and motor skills.

- Play group games such as Tag or Duck-Duck-Goose. These build listening skills, help children learn to follow directions, and provide much needed movement.
  - *Duck-Duck-Goose*

    Kids sit down in a circle facing each other. One person is "it" and walks around the circle. As this person walks around, he or she taps people's heads and says whether each is a duck or a goose. Once someone is the goose, he or she gets up and chases "it" around the circle. The goal is for the goose to tag the child that is "it" before "it" is able to sit down in the goose's spot. If the goose is not able to do this, the goose becomes "it" for the next round and play continues. If the goose does tag the "it" person, the person tagged has to sit in the center of the circle. Then the goose becomes "it" for the next round. The child in the middle can't leave until another person is tagged and he or she is replaced.

- Nesting boxes that can then be turned upside down to build towers are excellent, inexpensive materials for the four-year-old (Figure 4.6). On your list of school supplies, ask parents to send empty, sturdy, cardboard boxes in certain dimensions. Students can challenge themselves to see how high they can stack. (No competition, please!)

Figure 4.6   Stacking Blocks

For Social and Emotional Development

- Set up procedures for transition times in the classroom. Four-year-olds need security, and transitions may be difficult for them. As you switch from one activity to another, be sure to give accurate warning that this change will take place. Put on some transition music and tell the children that in a few minutes they will be moving to another area or beginning a new task.

- Continue to use the faces from Chapter 3 to help develop awareness of their own feelings and those of others.

- Use the dress up corner to increase this development. Have children dress up and pretend. As they act out scenarios, they will learn how to respond in different situations. Be prepared to coach appropriate behaviors!

- Continue to encourage pretend play through make-believe trips to the grocery store or pizza parlor. Have pretend birthday parties that the children help to plan.

For Cognitive Development

- Cut out pictures from magazines and have children sort them into different categories.

- Provide puzzles of 12–15 pieces.

- Have a puppet center, and let children put on puppet shows.

- Take "field trips" outside or around the building, and have children identify geometric shapes that they see.

- Work on concepts such as "over" and "under."

- Use the table and a stuffed animal. Put the animal under the table and ask the children where it is. Put it on the table. Beside the table. Have it jump over the table, etc. Or ask students to place themselves under the table, behind the table, etc.

- Work on similar prepositional concepts with this game: "Children, I am going to close my eyes and then tell you what I want you to do. When I open my eyes, I will see if you can follow my directions. Okay? Ready?" Close your eyes and say, "I want everyone to be standing next to the table." Then, "I want to see everyone sitting under the table." Continue with other commands to practice these concepts. My students loved these games. Those who don't understand the concepts will imitate the other children and eventually get it. Then you can have a student be the director.

- Provide pictures of objects and animals of different sizes. Have four-year-olds determine which are big and which are small (Figure 4.7).

Figure 4.7   Different Sizes

- Play with shapes! Have students draw or paint shapes like circles, squares, etc. Then ask what they can make with the shape. Model how to make something out of each shape (Figure 4.8).

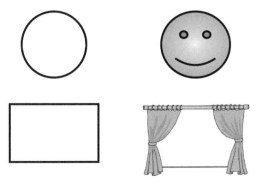

Figure 4.8   What Can You Make With Different Shapes?

- Have students find the shapes in different pictures or places.
  - ○ Find the circles and squares in the picture in Figure 4.9.
  - ○ How many rectangles can you find in our room?

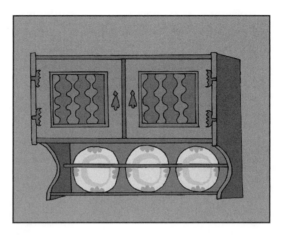

Figure 4.9   Find Shapes

- Read poems or stories using numbers.

Two Birds

There were two birds sitting on a stone.

One flew away, and then there was one.

The other bird flew after and then there was none,

And so the stone was left alone.

Brain Briefing

While visiting a nearby preschool, I noticed signs for parents:

No Cell Phones Allowed! It seems that parents would come to pick up their children and carry on conversations at the same time. Therefore, children were not greeted by their parents, and there was no dialogue about how the day went.

Child Development Checklist: Four-Year-Olds

Name _____   Grade _____

Birth date _____   Chronological Age _____

READING and LANGUAGE DEVELOPMENT

____ Very talkative

____ Vocabulary expanding

____ Uses complete sentences

____ Enjoys singing simple songs

____ Enjoys rhymes and nonsense words

____ May add "ed" to words

____ Adjusts language for the audience

____ Can spell name aloud

____ Can identify uppercase letters

Recommendations for increasing reading and language growth:

_____

_____

_____

PHYSICAL and MOTOR DEVELOPMENT

____ Climbs   ____ Skipping may be achievable

____ Swings   ____ Stands on one foot

____ Somersaults   ____ Hops

Fine motor skills:

____ Traces   ____ Builds

____ Draws   ____ Writes (scribbles)

____ Finger paints

Recommendations for increasing physical and motor growth:

_____

_____

_____

SOCIAL and EMOTIONAL GROWTH

____ May have an imaginary friend   ____ Is influenced by friends' behavior

____ May tattle or call others names   ____ Wants to please

____ Likes to sing, dance   ____ Active fantasy life

____ May still lie

____ Bases friendship on shared activities

____ Excludes children she doesn't like

Recommendations for increasing social and emotional growth:

_____

_____

_____

COGNITIVE GROWTH

____ Learns by doing

____ Can compare sets of items

____ Loves being read to

____ Can tell you his or her name, address, and phone number (near the end of the fourth year)

____ May be able to copy own name

____ Draws a person with basic large body parts (head, arms, legs, trunk)

____ Questions many things (death, sex, etc.)

____ Can count from five to seven items

____ Accurately names four or more colors

____ Likes to label and classify the environment

Recommendations for increasing cognitive growth:

_____

_____

_____

Figure 5.1   Jenna

The Five-
Year-Old Brain

Jenna is an active imaginative five-year-old (Figure 5.1). She is very athletic, as her mom has had her enrolled in gymnastics since she was three. Jenna loves to learn, but she wants to learn her way—through play and interaction.

Jenna tries to be helpful. She is always asking her teacher if she can put things away, get things out, run errands, and empty the wastebasket. At home, Jenna wants to set the table and dust the house.

She is calmer than she was as a four-year-old. Jenna takes life a bit more seriously, is very literal, and does what she is told. For instance, in her kindergarten class, the teacher told everyone to "not say a word." And Jenna was silent almost the whole day. When Miss Brown asked her what was the matter, Jenna lowered her head and said, "Is it okay to answer you? You said not to say a word." Miss Brown, a new teacher, learned her lesson that day when she realized she had made that request hours ago. The children had been unusually quiet since then, so she came to terms with the importance of the words she chose. Miss Brown started saying, "I need you all to be quiet *until I finish this story*," or "Don't make a sound *until. . . .*"

Jenna couldn't wait to go to kindergarten. Finally, she would be at "the big kids' school" with her older sister. Although Jenna enjoyed preschool, kindergarten seemed to be a whole new world for her. She was curious about playing with new children, and she loved getting on the bus!

Sometimes sitting still at school is a problem for five-year-olds. Toward the end of the fifth year, they may become more wiggly and jiggly (Wood, 1997) (Figure 5.2).

Figure 5.2 Jenna Working Out Her Wiggles

Miss Brown knows that her students have short attention spans, and she must keep things moving at a fast pace. However, she also knows that these children like routine and ritual. They must focus on one thing at a time.

> ***Brain Briefing***
>
> According to Hannaford (2005), there must be movement to anchor thought. Therefore, these seemingly short attention spans may be lengthened by adding movement to the learning. In some cases, that movement may be the fine motor movements involved in speech or writing. The neurotransmitter, acetylcholine, is released as neurons connect through speech and writing as well as through larger motor movement. This chemical aids in forming long-term memory.

BRAIN DEVELOPMENT

Important changes are taking place in the five-year-old brain. Some areas are continuing growth from the previous year, and we can look at changes in electrical activity and in memory.

1. Myelination of the corpus callosum of the frontal lobe continues (Kagan & Herschkowitz, 2004). A small increase in the short-term memory system called *immediate* or *conscious memory* may be seen. As more connections are made between the hemispheres at this part of the brain, understanding language and reading may be accelerated. Incoming information may be connected to prior knowledge more easily. Myelination begins in late fetal development and the early postnatal period, but it continues in the forebrain regions of humans through adolescence and into early adult life (Giedd et al., 2004). Development of white matter structure in children correlates with increased development of motor skills and reading ability and increased cognitive function (Casey, Giedd, & Thomas, 2000; Paus et al., 2001; Schmithorst et al., 2002). One can expect that five-year-olds will have the ability to plan and organize in a simple fashion.

2. The limbic system continues the myelination process (Kagan & Herschkowitz, 2005). The hippocampus and amygdala are creating greater connections to each other and to other areas of the brain. Now memories should become clearer as both the emotional aspect of the memory and the factual aspect can be connected.

3. Blood flow continues to be greater in the left hemisphere (Kagan & Herschkowitz, 2005). At this point in development, with proper experience, the five-year-old is expanding his or her vocabulary and comprehending more through dialogue. This vocabulary growth expands the connections in Wernicke's area and Broca's area, asking for more energy expenditure.

4. Dendritic complexity increases in order to facilitate the formation of memory (Herschkowitz & Herschkowitz, 2006). This dendritic growth may be due to experience; therefore, students will have diverse

memories and background knowledge. Along with the myelination of the limbic area, the growing dendrites may indicate the formation of new memories.

5. The left hemisphere shows an increase in dendritic growth in Broca's area (Eliot, 1999). This may be the final year of such massive growth, as by the age of six, most brains are showing a stronger dendritic pattern in the right hemisphere.

6. Electrical activity in the brain, as measured by an electroencephalogram, gains coherence between the ages of 4 and 6 (Kagan & Herschkowitz, 2005). Coherence is defined as neural activity that is synchronized. It is believed that when this occurs, the brain is better able to integrate the past with the present.

These changes are summarized in Figure 5.3.

LANGUAGE AND READING DEVELOPMENT

Five-year-olds love to carry on conversations. However, they may not share much information about what goes on at school. That's why those weekly letters home are important. When they do share, some information may be distorted. My principal always told the parents that if they believed only half of what the children told them about what happens at school, we would believe only half of what they told us about what goes on at home!

According to Elias and Arnold (2006), this may be the age when internal language develops. This is an important advancement, as reading comprehension relies on verbal and visual memory (Brookes, 2006).

Five-year-olds

- participate appropriately in conversations.

- listen carefully to unfamiliar sounds.

- love to be read to.

- know the parts of a book and their functions.

- begin to track print when listening to familiar text.

- use "would" and "could" appropriately.

- identify and name all uppercase and lowercase letters (Armistead, Duke, & Moses, 2005).

- have speech that is almost completely understandable.

- use longer sentences of seven or more words.

- enjoy copying letters, numbers, and designs.

- look at books and pretend to read (some may be reading).

- are using past tense more consistently.

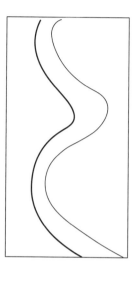

Corpus callosum continues to be myelinated between frontal lobes.

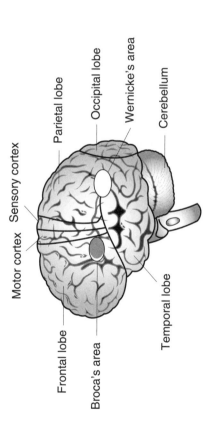

Motor cortex   Sensory cortex

Frontal lobe

Broca's area

Temporal lobe

Parietal lobe

Occipital lobe

Wernicke's area

Cerebellum

Broca's area shows more dendritic growth.

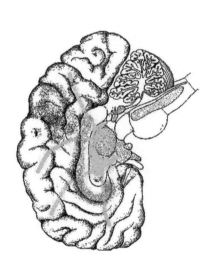

Coherence of electrical activity
Synchronization to integrate past with present.

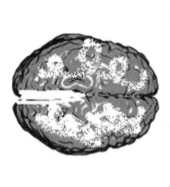

Increased dendritic complexity and connectivity between amygdala, hippocampus, and other brain areas.

Figure 5.3   Changes in a Five-Year-Old's Brain

> ***Brain Briefing***
>
> Some researchers suggest that age five is the end of the period for optimal physical and motor growth. Scientists believe that in this area, there may be a time when it is too late to make the perfect connections for ideal motor skills. Although the opportunity may extend itself to age eleven, it is important for adults to work with students on physical skills. Unfortunately, many believe that these skills are not learned, but rather hard-wired in the brain (Bergen, 2006).

PHYSICAL AND MOTOR DEVELOPMENT

Five-year-olds are still busy beings. Perhaps not able to leap tall buildings, they will nevertheless try to jump from table heights (Herr & Larson, 2004). They walk on their tiptoes, can do a broad jump, and try to ride a bicycle (usually with training wheels). Fine motor skills are improving in some areas, but keep in mind that there will be a vast continuum in this area. Free play is vital to development and learning. Recent studies suggest that children who learn through play do better in their later years in school (Ginsburg et al., 2007).

Five-year-olds

- walk a balance beam.
- may skip.
- go up and down stairs alternating feet.
- are getting better at running and jumping.
- have difficulty copying from the blackboard.
- use scissors and can cut on a line.
- try roller skating and ice skating.
- catch balls with their hands.

Five-year-olds' fine motor skills include

- holding a marker or pencil correctly.
- cutting and pasting.
- lacing their shoes.
- copying most letters.
- coloring within lines.
- copying square, triangle, and diamond shapes.
- printing their first names.

SOCIAL AND EMOTIONAL DEVELOPMENT

Five-year-olds are beginning to become competitive and develop a sense of fairness. Although winning isn't everything, they may verbally express anger when things don't go their way. Playing with older siblings is fun for five-year-olds, but as far as friends are concerned, they enjoy children of the same sex and age (Herr & Larson, 2004).

Five-year-olds

- often exclude other children in play—best friends only.
- prefer playing in small groups.
- protect younger children.
- respect other people's property.
- like to feel grown up; boast about themselves to younger, less capable children.
- understand and enjoy both giving and receiving.
- play well without adult supervision.
- need rules that are consistent and enforced for social behavior.

COGNITIVE DEVELOPMENT

Five-year-olds are creative as well as detail-oriented. They can make up their own original stories and retell in detail stories they have heard. Cause and effect become recognizable at this age. Between now and next year, five-year-olds will have an understanding of the number line. They will be able to add several sets of items and move up the number line. They may know that a set of five is less than a set of six and more than a set of four, which indicates an understanding of addition and subtraction.

Five-year-olds

- can count and compare.
- can add two sets by "counting on" (Hirsch-Pasek & Golinkoff, 2003).
- will give name and address when asked.
- think ahead, but not much more than a week or two.
- name the days of the week.
- recognize the numerals 1 to 5.
- use a vocabulary of 2000 or more words.
- write the numerals 1 to 10 by the end of the fifth year.

DEVELOPMENTALLY APPROPRIATE ACTIVITIES FOR FIVE-YEAR-OLD BRAINS

For Language and Reading Development

- Read aloud to the children every day.
- Read and ask "What if?" questions: Read "The Three Little Pigs," and ask, "What if there were four little pigs?"
- Read chapter books, and ask the children to predict what will happen.

- Partner reading is now possible; start with very familiar books. In partner reading, students partner up. One partner reads as the other checks for mistakes and fluency. Then they reverse roles.

- Build vocabulary through conversation as well as reading

- Buy magnetic strips and have five-year-olds write their favorite words on them. Then let them determine if any of the words rhyme. If not, can they come up with a rhyming word to record on a strip of magnetic tape? Other children can then "play" by trying to find the rhyming words and put them together.

- Storytelling is the bridge between language and reading (Hirsh-Pasek & Golinkoff, 2003). Get picture books that will stimulate storytelling.

- Read a story to the class, and then tell them it's their turn to read. Let students look at the pictures and continue the story. If it's a familiar story, they will stay with the plot, but if it's a new story, they may create some wonderful twists and turns.

- Discuss and draw pictures from the story: characters, setting, plot, etc.

- Read nonfiction and fiction books. Make sure students understand the difference.

- Collect postcards, and have children tell the story that the picture tells them.

- Begin to tell a story to the class. Stop after one or two sentences and let the children volunteer to continue the story.

- Play Silly Simon Sez. Silly Simon says words that rhyme with what the real word is. For instance, "Silly Simon says, touch your boulder." With that, touch your shoulder and say, "Is this a boulder? No. It's a shoulder!" Have all the children say the word together (Brookes, 2006).

Brain Briefing

Although technology, such as computers, has become an integral part of our curriculums, we must keep in mind that younger children need interaction with their peers and adults for learning. There is also the theory by Jane Healy (1998) that this is the age at which children should be producing their own visual images rather than having images given to them via computer, video, etc.

For Physical and Motor Development

- When children are pretend playing, have them write a grocery list if they are playing house, a prescription if they are doctors, a phone message, or a "Do Not Disturb" sign.

- Continue using obstacle courses outside or inside to fine-tune those gross motor skills.

- Play Pass the Ball

○ See how many different ways you can get a ball around a circle or the room. One person with the ball bounces it to another, and each successive player does the same. When the ball reaches the sender, the one next to the sender starts it in a different way—two hands, one hand, high, low, under leg, backwards, etc.

- Musical Chairs with a challenge: Say to the children, "When the music starts, everyone must move to the chair on the right." Stop the music and give another command with a direction. You don't have to take away chairs. This activity offers opportunities to develop movement skills, listening skills, and directional skills.

- Follow Me! This game involves a leader walking around the room and tapping several children on the shoulder. They get up and follow the leader until the leader goes back to his or her seat. Then the followers return quickly to their seats. The first one back is the new leader. Options: The leader may skip, hop, leap, etc.

- Five-year-olds are beginning to jump rope. Try jumping rope to a rhyme, and let the children jump and count as high as they can:
  My mother made a chocolate cake. How many eggs did it take?
  or
  Mabel, Mabel, neat and able
  Mabel, Mabel, set the table
  And don't forget the red hot peppers (children jump faster).

- Walk, gallop, run, and jump to various tunes.

For Social and Emotional Development

- Play Red Light–Green Light. If you do not remember this from playing it as a child, it goes like this: One person is "it" and gets to say either "red light" or "green light." Green light permits the other children to move. Red light indicates they must stand still. This is a great game for listening skills, gaining control over the body, and controlling impulses. When red light is announced, the person who moves first (before green light is said) will become "it." (You can add "yellow light" to warn them to slow down.)

Figure 5.4

- Work on the concept of "personal space." Use poster board, carpet squares, or anything you can to outline a personal space for each child. Talk about what they can do in their space (sit, lie down, jump?). Ask the five-year-olds how they feel about their own space and whether they are willing to share that space. How should they approach others about entering the others' personal space?

- Role-play and pretend play with a dress up corner that has hats, scarves, jackets, etc.

- Continue the activities from Chapter 4.

- Keep in mind that many five-year-olds are in kindergarten. This new experience calls for even more structure for security and safety.

- Assign classroom jobs. Make a chart and rotate tasks.

Brain Briefing

A University of Toronto study found that kids who have routine chores to do are likely to be more considerate of others (Grusec, Goodnow, & Cohen, 1997). Perhaps they feel that they are a part of something—that they "belong." This feeling offers them security, and they may feel safer as they comfort or help others.

For Cognitive Development

- Have lots of items for sorting by size, shape, and color.

- Use puzzles with 15 or more pieces

- Write about the family, neighborhood, community

- Encourage children to read everything in their environment: signs, labels, bulletin boards.

- Observe, talk, and write about nature.

- Practice writing numerals and letters.

- Check for knowledge of name, address, and phone number.

- Take apart a flashlight and see what is inside.

- Compare the needs of different living things.

- Make a collection such as of rocks, leaves, etc.

- Talk and read about changes in nature.

- Describe and present the differences between solids and liquids.

- Compare night and day.

- Explore the environment using thermometers, barometers, etc.

- Cook! Find very simple recipes, write them on a poster board, and have the children help you create. Remember that the recipe is a reading experience for the children as well as a source for building social skills such as taking turns. Keep the recipe up in the room, so they can refer to it and read the part they played in following the recipe (Kaltman, 2006).

- Change your bulletin boards and posters often. Put up thought-provoking and interesting pictures to talk about.

- Keep yourself inquisitive. This will help you develop curiosity in the students. Ask yourself "why" questions.

- Plant seeds. Teach the students how to take care of the plants and watch them grow.

- Play memory games with pictures of animals, people, or items to match. Then move on to word memory cards. Use simple words that the children can read and match.

- Invite guest speakers to come to class. Parents, grandparents, community members, and others can share their hobbies, experiences, or careers.

- Have students help write thank you notes to the guest speakers. This will help with reading, writing, and social skills.

- Have students create a map from home to school.

Brain Briefing

Many five-year-olds are attending full-day kindergarten. Keep in mind that even though these little bodies seem to constantly be on the go, they need rest. Their brains need rest. As learning takes place, neurons are communicating through the use of neurotransmitters. These carry electrical messages from one neuron to the next through the synaptic gap. The brain depletes itself of these chemicals when it is not allowed to rest between learning episodes. When this occurs, students become frustrated, as making connections is slower and more difficult (Willis, 2006).

Child Development Checklist: Five-Year-Olds

Name _____ Grade _____

Birth date _____ Chronological Age _____

LANGUAGE and READING DEVELOPMENT

____ Participates appropriately in conversations
____ Loves to be read to
____ Listens carefully to unfamiliar sounds
____ Uses "would" and "could" appropriately
____ Knows the parts of a book and their functions
____ Begins to track print when listening to familiar text
____ Identifies and names all uppercase and lowercase letters
____ Speech is almost completely understandable
____ Using longer sentences of seven or more words
____ Enjoys copying letters, numbers, and designs
____ Looks at books and pretends to read (some may be reading)
____ Using past tense is becoming more consistent

Recommendations for increasing reading and language growth:

_____

_____

_____

PHYSICAL and MOTOR DEVELOPMENT

____ Walks a balance beam   ____ Skips
____ Goes up and down stairs alternating feet ____ Catches ball with hands
____ Getting better at running and jumping   ____ Tries roller/ice skating
____ Uses scissors and can cut on a line

Fine motor skills:

____ Can hold a marker or pencil correctly   ____ Laces shoes
____ Can cut and paste   ____ Copies most letters
____ Copies square, triangle, and diamond shapes ____ Colors within lines
____ Prints first name

Recommendations for increasing physical and motor growth:

_____

_____

_____

SOCIAL and EMOTIONAL GROWTH

____ Often excludes other children in play—best friends only

____ Prefers playing in small groups

____ Protects younger children

____ Respects other people's property

____ Likes to feel grown up; boasts about self to younger, less capable children

____ Understands and enjoys both giving and receiving

____ Plays well without adult supervision

____ Needs rules that are consistent and enforced for social behavior

Recommendations for increasing social and emotional growth:

_____

_____

_____

COGNITIVE GROWTH

____ Can count and compare

____ Can add two sets by "counting on"

____ When asked will give name and address

____ Thinks ahead, but not much more than a week or two

____ Names the days of the week

____ Recognizes the numerals 1 to 5.

____ Uses a vocabulary of 2000 or more words

____ Writes the numerals 1 to 10 by the end of the fifth year.

Recommendations for increasing cognitive growth:

_____

_____

_____

Figure 6.1   Noah

The Six-
Year-Old Brain

Noah is six (Figure 6.1). Like most six-year-olds, Noah is competitive. He wants to be first in line for library at school, he wants to be first down to breakfast, and he wants to be picked first for group games. When Noah is not first, he can become a bad sport. For this reason, Noah's parents and teacher are working with Noah as personal/social/emotional coaches.

When Noah is not picked for a kick ball team at recess, he begins to yell at the other children and picks up the ball and throws it hard at his schoolmates.

Mrs. Washington checks to be sure the others aren't hurt and turns to have a conversation with Noah. It goes like this:

Mrs. Washington:	"Noah, I see that you are upset about the game. How do you feel about what has happened?"
Noah:	"I was at the playground first and I should have been picked to be on Jamar's team. Instead, I had to go on Tahlia's team. I don't want to be on a girl's team. I should have been picked first!"
Mrs. Washington:	"How does this make you feel?"
Noah:	"I'm mad. I won't play anymore."
Mrs. Washington:	"It must be difficult to play for a team when you don't want to. But, you know, sometimes I have to be on a committee at school when I don't want to."
Noah:	"So you quit, too?"
Mrs. Washington:	"No, Noah, I think that I might learn something if I stay on the committee. I have found that sometimes I really enjoy working with different people, and I learn a lot! Do you think this might happen with you on Tahlia's team?"
Noah:	"But I really want to be with Jamar. We sit next to each other and have fun."
Mrs. Washington:	"Noah, maybe you can tell Jamar about Tahlia's team. Explain how everyone played together and find out how his team played. If you join your team, you'll have information to share with him. If you don't, you might continue to be upset and that might not be fun for Jamar."
Noah:	"Okay, I'll try it. But Tahlia better do what I say."

This conversation ends with some hope that Noah will attempt to get along and be a better sport. His last words also are indicative of a six-year-old. Noah can be very bossy and critical. Mrs. Washington has her hands full with so many six-year-olds displaying the same behaviors. She makes it a point to spend time talking to the children about fairness, sportsmanship, and sharing authority. Six-year-olds can react to criticism in a negative way and can be easily discouraged.

The good news is that Noah is maturing, becoming more independent and is a bit daring (Figure 6.2).

Noah learns well through play. He likes to ask questions and finds himself tackling new tasks that may be a bit too difficult for him. Using games, riddles, poetry, and music are good ways to teach Noah.

As his curiosity leads him toward difficult tasks, Noah wants to know why things happen as well as how things happen. He will work long and hard on tasks, but perfection is not his goal. At this point quantity is more important than quality, so he needs encouragement to edit his work.

Figure 6.2   Noah is Maturing

BRAIN DEVELOPMENT

This is the beginning of logic and reason. Communication between the frontal lobes continues making it easier for the six-year-old to look at things from different viewpoints. This is an exciting time, as memory strategies begin to be understood and language and reading skills soar in many children.

1. Memory strategies begin to develop and be applied. Whereas younger children usually repeat information out loud over and over, six-year-olds may begin to use specific strategies to aid memory (Healy, 2004).

2. The anterior (front) corpus callosum continues to myelinate, making communication between the frontal lobes easier. Although the frontal lobes are not fully developed until the mid-20s, there is massive connectivity going on in the early years (Kagan & Herschkowitz, 2005).

3. The limbic system continues the myelination process (Kagan & Herschkowitz, 2005). The structures in the limbic system include the amygdala (the emotional center) and the hippocampus (the structure necessary for the creation of long-term memories).

4. The myelination process of the posterior (back) corpus callosum continues. Here the temporal and parietal lobes are linked. It is the temporal-parietal structure, Wernicke's area, that deals with word meaning and comprehension. As reading and vocabulary develop dramatically at this age, the connection between these lobes is vital (Eliot, 2007).

5. Dopamine levels in the prefrontal cortex are nearly at the same levels as in most adult brains. Focus and concentration rely on dopamine, as do attention and motivation. At this age, children begin to set long-term goals, and the prefrontal cortex is responsible for this behavior (Berk, 2006).

6. The reticular formation is generating new synapses and myelinating. Since this structure helps to maintain alertness and consciousness, improvement in attention and focus will be observed (Berk, 2006).

7. In brain imaging studies, growth in the tempo-parietal regions showed the highest growth rate in subjects ages 6 through 15 (Giedd et al., 2000).

These changes are summarized in Figure 6.3.

LANGUAGE AND READING DEVELOPMENT

By the age of six, most children have a vocabulary of between 10,000 and 13,000 words. Stories become more detailed, as six-year-olds add action, specifics, and drama. Since six-year-olds begin to understand rules, grammar rules make sense. The eyes are maturing to make reading easier, although copying from the board or from an overhead projector is still difficult. Some of this is because six-year-olds have a short working memory span. Remembering three to five words is an accomplishment. Remembering them long enough to transfer them to paper takes more time than their short-term memory has to hold such a large piece of information.

For instance, Noah tries to copy the sentence, "The boy ran to the store." He holds onto the first three words "The boy ran," but since he must hang on to these words for approximately 20 seconds, and he must also concentrate on printing them, he quickly loses the second or third word as he finishes the first. This memory process is stronger than it has ever been, but it will be a bit longer before copying is a simple task.

Six-year-olds

- are talkative.

- still love to be read to.

- can do some reading and writing.

- understand more complex grammar rules; use longer sentences.

- shift from learning by observing and experience to learning through language.

- use language to work through problems.

- listen carefully.

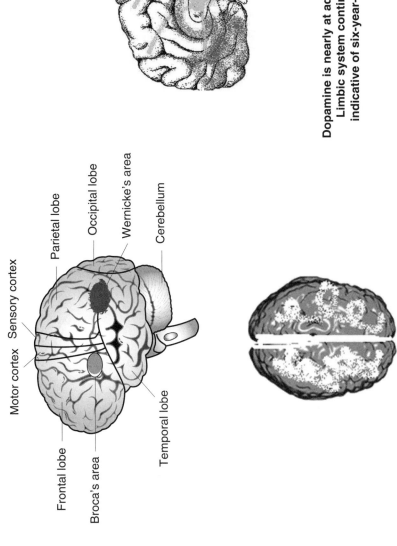

Dopamine is nearly at adult levels in the prefrontal cortex. Limbic system continues to wire up, which may be indicative of six-year-olds using memory strategies.

Motor cortex   Sensory cortex

Frontal lobe

Parietal lobe

Occipital lobe

Wernicke's area

Cerebellum

Broca's area

Temporal lobe

Posterior corpus callosum begins to be myelinated between parietal and temporal lobes.

Figure 6.3   Changes in a Six-Year-Old's Brain

> ### *Brain Briefing*
>
> Inner speech is very powerful. It slowly develops in the early years. By the time children are age six, the power of teaching promotes inner speech. Six-year-olds love to teach others, especially adults (Healy, 2004). According to David Sousa (2006), at some point in every lesson, the teacher should become the learner, and the learner should become the teacher. Provide opportunities for six-year-olds to teach each other and you. In doing so, they will use their inner speech to guide them through the step-by-step process.

PHYSICAL AND MOTOR DEVELOPMENT

Six-year-olds have energy. Even when they are sitting, many aren't sitting still. This is a tough time for some in school if their teachers have a lot of "seat work." Six-year-olds may be bouncing and moving while trying to follow the rules. My daughter, Marnie, used to fall off her chair as she wiggled around at her desk. As a result of increased brain development and experience, six-year-olds can accomplish quite a bit physically.

Six-year-olds

- stand on one foot with eyes closed for three seconds.
- skate.
- walk on a line in heel-toe fashion.
- skip with both feet.
- jump rope.
- ride a bicycle without training wheels.
- catch and bounce a tennis ball.
- can bounce a ball four to six times.

Six-year-olds' fine motor skills include

- drawing a diamond.
- cutting with a knife.
- holding a writing utensil with three fingers, with movement in the fingers.
- tying shoelaces.

SOCIAL AND EMOTIONAL DEVELOPMENT

According to Lillian Katz, "It is now very clear that unless a child reaches at least a minimal level of social competence by the age of six, he or she is at risk for the rest of his or her life" (as quoted in Dowling, 2005). The work of

Goleman (1995) and others has shown that social intelligence makes people more successful than general intelligence.

Even though six-year-olds are competitive creatures, rules still don't mean much to them. Watching them play competitive sports, like soccer, often leaves the parents aghast as they kick the ball into the opposing team's goal. And as they all try to kick the ball at the same time, no matter what their position, six-year-olds show their desire to win.

Six-year-olds

- are competitive.

- lack good sportsmanship.

- can be selfish.

- want good friends.

- may still throw tantrums.

- get upset when criticized.

Brain Briefing

Although many of the social and emotional characteristics of six-year-olds appear negative, this is an important time for good role models, emotional coaches, and communication between parents and teachers. Keep in mind that these youngsters are just beginning to develop some impulse control. When this system kicks in more, children will think about their selfishness, tantrums, and criticisms in a more mature manner. At this age, however, coaching students through these situations will help them make the connections to change their behaviors.

COGNITIVE DEVELOPMENT

Six-year-olds look at the world in a logical manner. They learn through discovery and begin to understand cause and effect. By age six or seven, children begin to reach adult levels of performance in areas requiring attention and impulse control (Bergen & Coscia, 2001). Six-year-olds attack their work. They are good starters but not necessarily strong finishers.

Six-year-olds

- ask many questions.

- see others' points of view (sometimes).

- value quantity of work more than quality.

- are good starters but don't always finish.

- can differentiate truth from fantasy.

- spontaneously group items.

- believe what they see to be true.

- give reasons.

- solve problems.

- can follow directions to make simple items.

- mix colors.

Brain Briefing

One of the most important components to a school day for children in their early years is routine. By setting up procedures, you free the working memory and prefrontal cortex to do higher-level thinking. Rather than clutter young minds with the question, "What do I do next?" procedures place an automatic response in the brain to many ordinary questions that would take up time and energy. The more the procedures are practiced, the more habitual they become. These also provide security in the classroom (Sprenger, 2007).

DEVELOPMENTALLY APPROPRIATE ACTIVITIES FOR SIX-YEAR-OLD BRAINS

For Language and Reading Development

- Read aloud to children every day.

- Play the Name Game: Go around the class, and ask each student to say his or her name. Then repeat the name, pausing between syllables and clapping each one out. Then ask children to join. ("Tommy/Tom [with a clap] my [with a clap]). Then go back around, clap out the syllables, and be sure the students can put the name back together. With a large class, do a few each day.

- Ask a different child each day to help you pick out what you will read aloud to the class. Provide different genres: poems, comics, stories, articles. Be sure to include nonfiction and real life texts, such as menus, directions, and instructions.

- Play Mystery Letters. Put students in pairs. Name one student in each pair as the writer and the other student as the paper. Have the paper's back to the writer's, so the writer can write letters on the paper's back. Have the paper close his or her eyes. Show the writers a letter to draw on the papers' backs. Tell the papers that they must try to picture in their minds the letter that is being drawn. After the writers write the letter, the papers either tell what the letter is or turn around and write the letter on the writer's back. This is great for the kinesthetic child. It helps with visualization and gives the teacher the opportunity for some informal assessment.

- Use a word wall: Put up to five new words each week on the word wall. As a class, practice saying the words, spelling the words, clapping out syllables, and breaking the words into phonemes. Here are more word wall activities: (1) Find two words that rhyme with ____. (2) Which word means _____? (3) Find words that end with ____.

- Play Taking Off: Using words from any story that you have read with your students, tell them that you are going to take off sounds. For instance, if you take off the *m* sound in mice, you get ice. Then go through several words from the story.

- Practice matching: Put several objects on a table. Ask a student to pick up one object and say its name. Have the other students say a rhyming word, say words with the same ending sound, or say words with the same beginning sound.

- Call children to line up by saying their names without the initial consonants. Then ask the class to tell what sound is missing.

- Use word sorts: These activities will enhance spelling and reading. (1) Closed sorts: Choose word categories, and give examples of words that fit each category. Have students sort the rest of the words from your list into the categories you chose. (2) Open sorts: Let students organize sets of words into their own categories.

- Use echo reading: Read a portion of text, and have the students repeat it or "echo" it back.

- Bring in magazines and newspapers. Challenge your students to find and circle the sight words they know on a page of a newspaper or magazine.

For Physical and Motor Development

- Have students walk, run, jump, hop, skip, gallop, slide, and leap around the gym, classroom, or playground as directed. Some skills can be performed forward and backward.

- Have students dribble a ball forward and backward around the designated play area. Have students throw, catch, and kick a ball with accuracy.

- Mimic movements found in different sports.

- Play the Hokey Pokey or the Chicken Dance.

- As six-year-olds are still learning left and right, play Simon Sez.

- Get six-year-olds started with basic physical activity. Teach them the proper way to do jumping jacks, push-ups, etc.

- Play jacks. Both boys and girls need the physical dexterity that this game offers. Teach them the rules and model the activity.

- Play Duck Duck Goose as described in Chapter 4.

- Play Pick Up Sticks for fine motor development.

Brain Briefing

Aerobic exercise is best for the brain. In one study, students who exercised intensely just three times per week performed better on classroom assignments than those who did not. Physical activity that does not raise the heart rate did not have the same effect. It appears that the minimum frequency of aerobic exercise necessary to get these benefits is three times per week (Rodriguez, 2007).

For Social and Emotional Development

- Start the day with a Feelings Circle, in which the students can express what they are feeling each day and why.

- Role-play different scenarios such as (1) How do you feel when someone criticizes your work? (2) How do you feel when you lose a game?

- Teach the rules of good sportsmanship.

- Help students create personal goals

- Create a "feelings word wall." Brainstorm feeling words with students and put them on the wall. Ask students at different times of day, "Which word describes how you are feeling?" Have students choose words and explain why they chose them. See if the explanation and word match. This will increase vocabulary and help students become aware of their feelings.

- Have students lie down and draw outlines of their bodies on butcher paper. Then have them cut out these figures and write on them what their strengths are. Then discuss weaknesses, and ask them to choose one to work on and strengthen, so they can add it to their outline.

- Practice "mind reading": Draw faces showing various emotional expressions. Have students examine each face, make their faces look like it, and describe the feeling. Explain that there are causes for people's feelings. Let them make up stories about the faces and why these people feel this way (Figure 6.4).

Figure 6.4   Sample Faces for "Mind Reading"

> ### *Brain Briefing*
>
> Children will rise to the level of the beliefs of their teachers (Siegel, 2007). Teachers who believe their students are gifted hold students to the expectation that they have the ability to achieve. In studies, this has proven to be accurate. When teachers were told that their classes were a combination of gifted and learning disabled students, they raised expectations for the gifted students, and those students performed up to expectations. Later teachers discovered that these gifted students were actually learning disabled.

For Cognitive Development

- Discuss different rehearsal strategies for remembering. Be sure students can explain the strategy as well as use it. Better memory performance results if the students can explain their strategy.

- Provide students with lots of opportunity for measuring. Water tables and sand tables are useful.

- Teach new concepts in a multimodal way, using visual, auditory, and kinesthetic approaches. Six-year-olds need movement.

- Play games with simple logic.

- Play charades. Use cards with pictures if you have emergent readers. Let the students act out the word or scene they have.

- Give students the opportunity to match and sort items. Collect caps of all kinds—toothpaste caps, jar caps, bottle caps, etc.—ask parents to send some to school. Use them for students to sort. They can be sorted by size, type, the letter they start with, whether you can stack them, etc.

- Make connections. Give students worksheets with two columns of items, and have them draw lines from an item on the left to something that it connects to on the right. Give the students the opportunity to explain how the items relate to each other.

Brain Briefing

According to Sylwester (2007), the sensory lobes, which first recognize challenge and then analyze it, mature in these early years. Appropriate responses to these challenges may not mature until adolescence and early adulthood.

This is certainly not the end of the early years, but this poem by A. A. Milne offers a nice summary of what it is like to be a six-year-old.

The End

When I was One,

I had just begun.

When I was Two,

I was nearly new.

When I was Three,

I was hardly Me.

When I was Four,

I was not much more.

When I was Five,

I was just alive.

But now I am Six, I'm as clever as clever.

So I think I'll be Six now for ever and ever.

—A. A. Milne

Child Development Checklist: Six-Year-Olds

Name _____ Grade _____

Birth date _____ Chronological Age _____

READING and LANGUAGE DEVELOPMENT

____ Talkative

____ Still loves to be read to

____ Can do some reading and writing

____ Understands more complex grammar rules

____ Uses longer sentences

____ Shifts from learning by observing and experience to learning through language

____ Uses language to work through problems

____ Listens carefully

Recommendations for increasing reading and language growth:

_____

_____

_____

PHYSICAL and MOTOR DEVELOPMENT

____ Stands on one foot with eyes closed for three seconds

____ Walks on line in heel-toe fashion

____ Skips with both feet

____ Jumps rope

____ Rides bicycle without training wheels

____ Catches and bounces tennis ball

____ Can bounce a ball four to six times

Fine motor skills

____ Draws diamond   ____Ties shoelaces

____ Holds writing utensil with three fingers
with movement in the fingers

Recommendations for increasing physical and motor growth:

_____

_____

_____

SOCIAL and EMOTIONAL GROWTH

____ Competitive

____ Lacks good sportsmanship

____ Can be selfish

____ Wants good friends

____ May still throw tantrums

____ Becomes upset when criticized

Recommendations for increasing social and emotional growth:

_____

_____

_____

COGNITIVE GROWTH

____ Asks many questions

____ Sees others' points of view (sometimes)

____ Values quantity of work more than quality

____ Is a good starter but doesn't always finish

____ Can differentiate truth from fantasy

____ Spontaneously groups items

____ Believes what he or she sees to be true

____ Can follow directions to make simple items

____ Gives reasons

____ Solves problems

____ Mixes colors

Recommendations for increasing cognitive growth:

_____

_____

_____

Figure 7.1   Jordan

The Seven-
Year-Old Brain

Enjoy Jordan's smile; his teacher tells me that he is a much happier seven-year-old than he was as a six-year-old. Jordan can be moody and he has some fears, but in general, he is a happy child (Figure 7.1).

You see, seven-year-olds worry. Jordan worries that his stomachache may be a serious illness. He is afraid he will be late for school. Many seven-year-olds are afraid of the dark.

Jordan is also a planner. If things go according to schedule, he is much more contented. He meets challenges head on and sticks with them. He has friends, but he prefers dealing with them one at a time. Jordan is independent, yet sensitive to others (Figure 7.2).

Seven-year-olds often seek perfection. Their work is a labor of love, and there can be many "do-overs." Jordan works slowly and always finishes what he starts, but he may erase his paper till he has created a hole. Then he starts over.

Fortunately for Jordan, his parents and his teacher are patient and kind. Mrs. Delgado loves her class and knows that she must work with the diverse emotions of this age. As the school year progresses, she will see her students as happy learners.

Jordan also loves Mrs. Delgado. Seven-year-olds tend to have personal relationships with their teachers. They like to stand close to them and may even hold the teacher's hand. Seven-year-olds like to bring things from home to share, but don't count on them for bringing notes or taking home newsletters.

Figure 7.2   Jordan and Friends

BRAIN DEVELOPMENT

What's going on inside Jordan's head? From the noisy six-year-old, the child becomes the sensitive and serious seven-year-old. This brain is completing the "five to seven" shift. Some of this shifting appears to be environment dependent.

1. The synaptic density in the frontal lobes peaks (Bergen & Coscia, 2001). Pathways of vertical control from the frontal lobes to the limbic system lead to better impulse control, greater independence, improved ability to plan, and the acceptance of responsibility. It is evident that some children do not form these networks that allow the prefrontal cortex to connect to the limbic area, and as a result, these children may be at risk (Elias & Arnold, 2006).

2. Glucose production remains high and will continue at this high level for the next year or two (Kagan & Herschkowitz, 2005). The total surface of the cortex has been increasing since the age of two. It will continue to need high energy as this area expands.

3. Dopamine levels continue to rise. This neurotransmitter is released as goals become attainable. Therefore, seven-year-olds should be able to set and reach goals. Motivation and attention rely on dopamine as well (Berk, 2005; Kagan & Herschkowitz, 2005).

4. Growth in Broca's area is greater in the right hemisphere after age six, indicating that this hemisphere is contributing to the emotional and prosodic components of language. This means that such things as irony and sarcasm begin to be understood. Reading fluency will be affected as well (Kagan & Herschkowitz, 2005).

5. Myelination of the posterior corpus callosum connecting the temporal and parietal lobes continues to increase (Kagan and Herschkowitz, 2005).

6. The brain continues to increase its massive interconnectedness (Bergen, 2007). Next year, at the end of early childhood, this interconnectedness will be complete. That is not to say that the brain doesn't keep making connections but rather that the brain will be 90 percent of its adult weight and will be prepared for the next massive change occurring during adolescence. The growth from three to eight is a slow growth; from eight to twelve the growth is accelerated.

These changes are summarized in Figure 7.3.

Brain Briefing

Adults who acquire a second language before this age can gain complete mastery without compromise to either language (Sleeper, 2007). Sometime between the seventh and twelfth year, a second language uses different sites in Broca's area for the new language. Before the seventh year, the first and second languages utilize the same site.

LANGUAGE AND READING DEVELOPMENT

Seven-year-olds still like the teacher to read books aloud. They learn new words and meanings quickly, and they understand concepts such as time and space. Since they don't like to make mistakes, seven-year-olds listen very carefully and speak articulately.

Seven-year-olds

- should handle opposite analogies easily: girl-boy, man-woman, flies-swims, blunt-sharp, short-long, sweet-sour, etc.

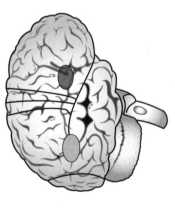

Broca's area in the right hemisphere is more active than in the left.

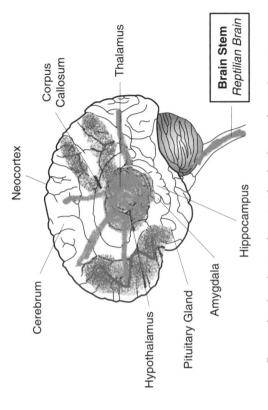

Neocortex

Corpus Callosum

Thalamus

Cerebrum

Hypothalamus

Pituitary Gland

Amygdala

Hippocampus

Brain Stem
Reptilian Brain

Dopamine levels continue to rise in the prefrontal cortex. Limbic system continues to wire up to the prefrontal cortex. Control over emotions becomes stronger.

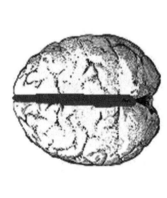

Myelination of the posterior corpus callosum continues to increase between parietal and temporal lobes.

Figure 7.3   Changes in a Seven-Year-Old's Brain

- understand such terms as alike, different, beginning, end, etc.

- should be able to do simple reading and to write or print many words.

- have rapidly expanding vocabularies.

- grow in their ability to understand abstract words and concepts (Eide & Eide, 2006).

According to Shaywitz (2003), between the ages of seven and eight, children link letters to sounds in order to decode words they don't know. They begin to learn strategies for breaking words into syllables. They begin to read with fluency. Both nonfiction and fiction are read and comprehended if at grade level. They read on their own because they want to and they represent the complete sound of a word when spelling it.

Brain Briefing

Language milestones are commensurate with the development and maturation of the language areas in the brain. Wernicke's area, which is associated with receptive language, matures before the expressive language locale, Broca's area (Eliot, 2007).

PHYSICAL AND MOTOR DEVELOPMENT

Motor maturity is obvious as seven-year-olds plan their movements ahead of time and practice their skills. The ability to follow rules makes game playing more rewarding. Keep in mind that seven-year-olds still rely on adult supervision. The drive to be perfect reaches all aspects of development at this serious age.

Seven-year-olds

- now have well-established hand-eye coordination and are likely to be more interested in drawing and printing.

- will practice and repeat skills.

- are aware of direction and distance.

- jump, leap, swim, bike, and ride scooters.

- plan their movements.

SOCIAL AND EMOTIONAL DEVELOPMENT

Seven-year-olds are a contradiction. Sometimes they seem to be happy being miserable. Other times, they are empathetic, interested, and gracious. As they reach for independence and start really thinking about themselves, it appears as though they are planning, thinking, and sorting things out.

Emotions seem to be under control when there are routines and schedules. Time is important, as they must finish what they start. They can be very sensitive, and if one child in class is mean to another, then a seven-year-old may think everyone is mean.

Seven-year-olds

- may cry easily.

- are moody.

- want one friend at a time.

- enjoy being alone.

- are affectionate.

- are polite and sympathetic.

- are becoming aware of their own emotions.

Brain Briefing

To promote a feeling of belonging in the classroom, assigning chores is important. Children who feel they are necessary to the running of the classroom will feel they are a part of it and be more willing to come to school and interact with other children (Sprenger, 2007).

COGNITIVE DEVELOPMENT

Seven-year-olds begin to use semantic categories. Relationships of concepts that are in different categories become clear to them. They understand that properties are not necessarily permanent. For instance, in comparing two glasses, both five-year-olds and seven-year-olds can tell which is bigger and which is smaller. But if the smaller glass is then compared to an even smaller glass, like a shot glass, the seven-year-old knows the once smaller glass is now the bigger glass.

Seven-year-olds

- can now relate several ideas simultaneously in their heads.

- understand the concept of numbers.

- know daytime and nighttime.

- know right and left hands.

- can copy complex shapes, such as a diamond.

- can understand commands with three separate instructions.

- can explain objects and their use.

- can repeat three numbers backwards.

- can read age-appropriate books or other materials.

- are upset if they cannot finish a task.

- should be able to tell time to the quarter hour.

Brain Briefing

Synapse production in the frontal lobe reaches its peak around the age of seven or eight (Eliot, 2007).

DEVELOPMENTALLY APPROPRIATE ACTIVITIES FOR SEVEN-YEAR-OLD BRAINS

For Language and Reading Development

- Read aloud daily to your students.

- Assess your students' phonemic awareness

- Play Alphabet War: Remember the card game War? Create enough decks of cards for each pair of students in class. Put one word on each card. They may be vocabulary words or words from a recent story or sight words. Partner the students and have them shuffle and divide the cards evenly. Then, at the same time, each partner turns a card face up. The person who has the word that comes first alphabetically wins the hand and collects the cards. The one with the most cards wins.

- Create a leveled library: The leveled library is a resource center of sets of leveled books that you can use with small groups of students to provide instruction in reading skills, fluency, and comprehension through guided reading.

- Practice rhyming: Provide a word, and ask each student to come up with a rhyming word.

- Make compound words: You provide the first part, and let students think of a second part that works, or you provide the first word and some options for which they may choose to go with it to make a compound word (Figure 7.4).

- Keep in mind that seven-year-olds hate mistakes. Allow them practice time and editing time for their work.

- Get the book *CDC* by William Steig. Give students a chance to read it. Ask them to open to any page and read. Discuss the difficulty with reading with expression, accuracy, and at a level rate.

Which word goes with flag ____?

    a. ship
    b. pole
    c. stag

Which word goes with grand ____?

    a. hall
    b. line
    c. son

Which word goes with high ____?

    a. way
    b. building
    c. tree

Which word goes with no ____?

    a. turn
    b. fair
    c. body

Which word goes with base ____?

    a. face
    b. ball
    c. tall

Figure 7.4   Making Compound Words

Brain Briefing

Both fine and gross motor skills are developing, but gross motor skills are still maturing at a faster pace. The cerebellum is increasing its ability to navigate both physical and cognitive skills. As the frontal lobes continue to develop, they will interact more with the cerebellum to plan more complex activities (Sylwester, 2007).

For Physical and Motor Development

- Play chess, checkers, or other strategy games.

- Run relay races; play hopscotch.

- Teach basketball rules and play.

- Throw and kick for accuracy.

- Do the Hokey Pokey and Chicken Dance.

- Teach fitness exercises.

- Teach aerobic exercise.

- Jump rope.
  - *Coffee and Tea*

    The jumping student chants, "I like coffee, I like tea, I'd like [name of next person in line] to come in with me." Then the two jump together, the second person saying the rhyme. When the rhyme is done, the first person runs out, and the new person comes in and jumps with the second person.

  - *Tiny Tim*

    I had a little puppy;
    His name was Tiny Tim.
    I put him in the bathtub, to see if he could swim.
    He drank all the water; he ate a bar of soap;
    The next thing you know he had a bubble in his throat.
    In came the doctor [person jumps in];
    In came the nurse [person jumps in];
    In came the lady with the alligator purse [person jumps in].
    Out went the doctor [person jumps out];
    Out went the nurse [person jumps out];
    Out went the lady with the alligator purse [person jumps out].

For Social and Emotional Development

- Continue working on emotional awareness using the faces from Chapter 6.

- Give seven-year-olds the opportunity to work with and teach younger children, as this may increase self-confidence.

- Role-play scenarios where students deal with their frustrations over mistakes or shyness.

- Discuss the emotions of characters in stories or poetry.

- Greet all students by name when they enter your classroom.

- Begin and/or end the school day with brief periods of time for students to reflect on what they have learned recently and what they might want to learn next. This lets them know you care about how they feel about their learning. It also gives them a chance to recall what was learned during the day.

- Seven-year-olds will learn and follow rules. Create rules in the classroom that recognize positive behavior. Include cooperation, caring, helping, encouragement, and support. Be sure that discipline rules and procedures are clear, firm, fair, and consistent.

- Show interest in students' personal lives outside the school. You may be the only adult who they believe cares.

- Ask them what kinds of learning environments have been most and least successful for them.

> **Brain Briefing**
>
> According to Vygotsky, children who work cooperatively and learn with others will ultimately learn to work on their own. Although seven-year-olds may have good social skills in general, some will not socialize without encouragement and must be taught the skills of sharing and taking turns (Dowling, 2005).

For Cognitive Development

- Ask many thought-provoking questions.

- Stimulate thinking with open-ended stories, riddles, thinking games, and discussions.
    - Try a book like Marilyn Helmer's *Yucky Riddles* (Toronto, ON: Kids Can Press, 2003).
    What goes ha, ha, ha, plop?
        Someone laughing his or her head off
    What did the vampire say when he saw the Count Dracula movie?
        That was fang tastic!

- Give students many opportunities for decision making and selecting what they would do in particular situations.

- Add stories that deal with reality. Provide biographies to read.

- Allow lots of time for tasks, to make sure students can complete them.

- Ask students to evaluate situations from different points of view.

- Provide positive reinforcement whenever possible.

- Play fun review games like $10,000 Pyramid or Password: Put students in teams of two. Show one player a list of words. This player must give the partner clues to the words without saying each exact word. Movements are allowed. The first team in which the player says all of the words wins. This is great for vocabulary review!

- Give students portions of text or short poems to memorize. This will increase working memory and allow them to practice rehearsal strategies.

> **Brain Briefing**
>
> Seven-year-olds are learning about their inner selves. As a result they are sometimes serious and somewhat sensitive. That's why reflection time is important for them. They are truly an enjoyable group of children. Their teacher must overlook some of the moodiness and focus on their wonderful developing brains. They still want to play, but they enjoy learning in various ways. They can make themselves sick with worry, so try to provide predictability to calm their brains (Sprenger, 2007).

Child Development Checklist: Seven-Year-Olds

Name _____ Grade _____

Birth date _____ Chronological Age _____

LANGUAGE and READING DEVELOPMENT

____ Should handle opposite analogies easily: girl-boy, man-woman, flies-swims, blunt-sharp, short-long, sweet-sour, etc.

____ Understands such terms as alike, different, beginning, end, etc.

____ Should be able to do simple reading and to write or print many words

____ May have doubled the size of listening and speaking vocabularies within the past year

____ Begins to learn strategies for breaking words into syllables

____ Begins to read with fluency

____ Reads and comprehends both nonfiction and fiction if at grade level

Recommendations for increasing reading and language growth:

_____

_____

_____

PHYSICAL and MOTOR DEVELOPMENT

____ Now has well-established hand-eye coordination and is likely to be more interested in drawing and printing

____ Will practice and repeat skills

____ Is aware of direction and distance

____ Jumps, leaps, swims, bikes, and rides scooters

____ Plans movement

Recommendations for increasing physical and motor growth:

_____

_____

_____

SOCIAL and EMOTIONAL GROWTH

____ May cry easily

____ Moody

____ Wants one friend at a time

____ Enjoys being alone

____ Fearful of many things

____ Complains

____ Feels that others are picking on him

____ Is becoming aware of his own emotions

Recommendations for increasing social and emotional growth:

_____

_____

_____

COGNITIVE GROWTH

____ Can now relate several ideas at the same time in his or her head

____ Understands concept of numbers

____ Knows right and left hands

____ Can copy complex shapes, such as a diamond

____ Can understand commands with three separate instructions

____ Can explain objects and their use

____ Can repeat three numbers backwards

____ Can read age-appropriate books and other materials

____ Becomes upset if he or she cannot finish a task

Recommendations for increasing cognitive growth:

_____

_____

_____

Figure 8.1   Alayna

The Eight-
Year-Old Brain

S ay hello to Alayna (Figure 8.1). When the going gets tough, eight-
year-olds get going. They are just as pleasant as they were at seven, and now
we find them even more outgoing. In fact, "exuberant" describes Alayna best.

Like other eight-year-olds, Alayna likes to evaluate. The one she judges
most is herself. She adores her mother and father and often sits in on or acci-
dentally overhears their conversations. She is waiting to hear what is said about
her. She hopes to hear praise, but she is also old enough to realize that her
parents have their own lives and may not spend time discussing her.

Alayna's feelings are easily hurt, but in general, she feels pretty good about herself. She may accomplish a task and seek positive reinforcement by saying something like, "This isn't very good. I better do it over," hoping this remark will lead to a positive comment about the job she did. However, Alayna is mature enough to know the difference between a real compliment and a false one.

Alayna is very wrapped up in her mother. She wants to please her and worries that she won't. Alayna's evaluative nature, however, will make her critical of her mother as well. This leads to a complicated relationship. Because her relationship with Dad is less intense, they seem to get along better than she and Mom. Despite the lack of affection Alayna has for her father, she respects and admires him. She will obey him better than she does Mom.

Eight-year-olds love to go to school. They are gregarious and don't want to miss anything. Alayna likes to bring things home from school. She will deliver the newsletter or teacher notes unfailingly. Eight-year-olds are simply less forgetful.

Alayna likes her teacher, Mrs. Garrison, but she likes even better to catch her teacher misspelling a word or leaving words out on a test. That evaluative nature is not put off by authority figures (Figure 8.2).

Although Alayna enjoys her schoolwork and gets along well, many eight-year-olds find third grade to be very difficult. At this level there are often fewer directions given, and students must think for themselves.

Figure 8.2 Alayna and Friend

> ### *Brain Briefing*
>
> The brain is designed the way a beautiful sculpture is made. It begins with more material than needed (connections), and only what is used and needed remains as the rest is pruned away. In my workshops, I often make and use my own play-dough for various hands-on activities. I begin by asking my participants to take a chunk of dough and tell them they are about to make a sculpture. As they look at their chunk, I tell them they might need more material to work with. They add more dough. We then look it over again. It still needs more. Finally, after adding several times, I tell them they are ready. Now they start taking away the dough to create a shape of a brain.

BRAIN DEVELOPMENT

The end of early childhood is certainly not the end of brain development. Rather it is a time for graduation, as the brain will begin to change in a different way. The early years provide the brain the time to create the interconnectedness necessary for all brain areas to communicate with each other. Now that this massive interconnectedness has taken place, or will have by the end of the eighth year, the brain is ready to take on new challenges.

The brain begins by becoming connected throughout. In this way there is more than enough material. As the adolescent grows and gets involved in different experiences, the brain is sculpted. Unused portions are pruned away and what remains is a designer brain!

1. White matter now exceeds gray matter due to the substantial interconnectedness of the brain (Kagan & Herschkowitz, 2005). That white matter is the myelin-coated axons that are capable of sending messages throughout the brain and body.

2. Accelerated growth of the prefrontal cortex begins (Kagan & Herschkowitz, 2005). During the early childhood phase, growth has been slow and steady. Now it will begin to accelerate as the brain prepares for the adolescent changes.

3. The brain reaches 90 percent of its adult weight by the end of the eighth year (Kagan & Herschkowitz, 2005). Glucose uptake, which has been very high, will now begin to decline until it reaches adult levels at 18 or 20.

4. Organization for memory begins (Berk, 2005). This mature early childhood brain has begun to store memories and memory strategies. The key to strong long-term memory storage is organization. What allows the brain to concentrate on memory is that so many procedures, such as reading and writing, have become automatic. When eight-year-olds don't have to focus on decoding words or how to print or write their letters, the brain is free to focus on content and comprehension.

> ### Brain Briefing
>
> Many eight-year-olds are using memory strategies. There are times when they must be encouraged to do so. For instance, visualizing a scene from a story is an excellent way of remembering. Some children have trouble visualizing and may need to draw pictures (Eide & Eide, 2006).

5. The brain strengthens its abilities for learning as myelination of fibers speeds association between senses and ideas (Healy, 2004). Information enters our brains through our senses. As connections between sensory areas and association areas increase, the areas for higher-level thinking become stronger, and information processing accelerates.

These changes are summarized in Figure 8.3.

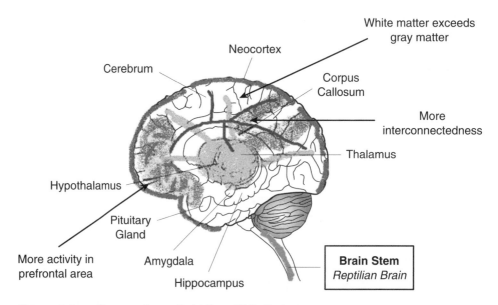

Figure 8.3   Changes in an Eight-Year-Old's Brain

LANGUAGE AND READING DEVELOPMENT

Eight-year-olds have entered a different world of reading. Caution must be taken here, as not all eight-year-olds are reading at the same level. In third grade, however, students are expected to learn from their reading. The switch from developmental reading to content-area reading approaches. Teachers must keep in mind that all literacy is language based. In other words, no matter what content you are teaching, it has its own literacy that you must teach. So, as you begin to teach science, keep in mind that your students may not have the reading skills for that particular literacy. You must model how to read that content and assist students with reading difficulties.

Eight-year-olds

- are replacing learning to read with reading to learn (Healy, 2004).

- can relate rather involved accounts of events, many of which occurred at some time in the past.

- can easily use complex and compound sentences.

- have few lapses in grammatical constructions.

- have established all speech sounds, including consonant blends.

- should be reading with considerable ease and writing simple compositions.

- should know and use social amenities in speech in appropriate situations.

- have established control of rate, pitch, and volume in reading aloud.

- can carry on conversation at a rather adult level.

- follow fairly complex directions with little repetition.

Brain Briefing

Brain growth and changes continue throughout our lives. But some research suggests that by age eight or nine, there will be limited synaptic growth in some areas of the brain (Bergen, 2006).

PHYSICAL AND MOTOR DEVELOPMENT

It is now much easier to copy from the board. Visual acuity is good, and it is no longer laborious to switch from the board to the paper. Working memory has increased as well, so more can be held in memory as eight-year-olds copy the material. Team sports are important for this age group. Emphasis must be based on exercise, social interaction, and having a good time rather than on competition.

Eight-year-olds

- wiggle and clown around.

- make faces.

- may have accidents due to so much activity.

- need physical activity every day, approximately 30 minutes.

- perform in much the same way as seven-year-olds.

SOCIAL AND EMOTIONAL DEVELOPMENT

Some eight-year-olds are actually getting ready for puberty. Therefore, there may be some emotional reactions that are unexpected, as hormones begin to play a part in the bodies of eight-year-olds—in particular, girls.

Having a personal space at home and at school may be important to many children of this age. A cubby hole or locker at school, and/or a lock box or a locked drawer at home make many eight-year-olds feel they have the privacy they desire.

Eight-year-olds are often found giggling over things like dirty jokes. This preadolescent behavior shows up in many.

Eight-year-olds

- articulate their feelings.

- may keep secrets.

- tend to dramatize.

- may be sensitive.

- eventually obey, but may begin with resistance.

- like instant gratification and positive reinforcement.

- usually are affectionate, helpful, cheerful, outgoing, and curious, but can also be rude, demanding, silly, and bossy.

- make new friends easily and work at establishing good two-way relationships.

- may develop a close friend of the same sex.

- consider clubs and groups important.

- enjoy school, don't like to be absent, and tend to talk more about it.

- are somewhat possessive of their things.

COGNITIVE DEVELOPMENT

According to child development expert Dr. Laura Berk (2005), at this age students are aware of and are using attentional strategies. Since emotion drives attention, and attention drives learning and memory, it is important to keep the classroom safe and predictable (Sylwester, 2003).

Eight-year-olds

- want to know the reasons for things.

- can retell a story with events in the right order.

- begin to find math useful.

- need skills and rituals that lay a solid base for moving on to new challenges.

- see many points of view.

- realize that doing well depends on paying attention.

- have well-developed time and number concepts.

DEVELOPMENTALLY APPROPRIATE ACTIVITIES FOR EIGHT-YEAR-OLD BRAINS

For Language and Reading Development

- Read aloud every day.

- Fun and movement to learn verbs: Write verbs on large cards. Use words like running, skipping, bouncing, slithering, standing, sitting, etc. Show the verb to four or five students at one end of the room, and have them perform the action. Ask the rest of the group to guess the verb. This is great fun, can increase vocabulary, and provides blood and oxygen to the brain.

- Write letters to characters in stories.

- Write letter to authors.

- Write and illustrate a book like one of the books just read. It might have a similar plot line, setting, or characters. You can share the pen, so that all the children become coauthors, and each adds to the story.

- Have students write in journals. They may draw as well. They might use this writing time to report what they have learned, reflect on new concepts, or do free writing.

- Read stories and ask for points of view of different characters, for example, Little Red Riding Hood from the wolf's point of view, or Charlotte's Web from Templeton's point of view.

- Ask students to choose one of the following categories to write about: pets, vacation, school, or sports. Then give them a few minutes to think of their story. It may be fact or fiction. Group the students according to the categories they choose. In small groups, have children tell the gist of their story in about one or two minutes. Then each group member must write three questions they would like answered about the story. Each child is given the questions and may use them to expand the story. This promotes listening skills and thinking skills, and it helps children add details and support to their writing.

For Physical and Motor Development

- Everyone Tags Everyone: In a big space that's safe to run around in, start with one person as "It." "It" runs around and tries to tag everyone else. When "It" tags someone, that person joins "It" in hunting for new people to tag. The game is over when there's no one left to tag because everyone is "It."

- Freeze Tag is by far the most widely used variation of Tag. In this game, "It" turns the other players to ice and makes them hold still. To start, give the children a second to scatter before "It" takes off after them. When "It" touches them, they must freeze. There they stay, unable to move until an unfrozen player is able to tag them. This "melts" the ice and allows them to move. The game's over when "It" has frozen all the players. Since "It" must not only chase down its opponents but also guard its victims, "It" gets quite a workout, and the game goes on for longer than most other forms of Tag.

- Freeze Tag variation: If you find the game takes too long with players waiting to get unfrozen, change the rules so that the freeze is irreversible.

- Most early learning standards in physical education require that students be aware of rules of many types of sports and games. Post those rules to help reinforce them.

- Promote following instructions by asking eight-year-olds to do things like jog around the gym, dribble the basketball up and down the court twice, or throw the ball to three people before they put it away (Woodfield, 2004).

- Encourage and insist upon cooperation in sports. Relay races are one way of using cooperation.

- Have timed races with students competing only against their own times. Provide charts that they can use to keep track.

- Have the following equipment available:
  - Various balls: a soccer ball, volleyball, playground ball, basketball
  - Hula-hoops
  - Jump ropes
  - Frisbees
  - Balance beam
  - Poster with proper stretching techniques

Brain Briefing

The first ten years of life are dedicated to the development of the sensory lobes while the second ten years show great development of executive functions in the frontal lobe (Sylwester, 2007). Frontal lobe development is blossoming in the eight-year-old in preparation for higher levels of thinking and planning. It is imperative that during early childhood, students practice problem-solving and social emotional skills.

For Social and Emotional Development

- Encourage students to name their own feelings and identify the feelings of others.

- Use the Emotional Bingo cards in the book *Wanna Play?* by Ross and Pacchione (2007). This game allows students to develop their skills at identifying emotions in others.

- Provide a personal space for each child. Explain the concept of personal space. My colleague Margo Miller used 12-by-18-inch pieces of construction paper. She placed them on the floor, one for each student, about two feet apart. Everyone stood on a "space." She emphasized that each student deserved to have his or her own personal space and that they should not get any closer than they currently were without being invited. It really worked!

- Share personal experiences with the students, and ask them to share some of theirs. Ask the students how they felt after hearing about these experiences. Discuss the concept of empathy.

- Try not to criticize. Encourage efforts. Teach that others also make mistakes. Sometimes I would purposely make mistakes when writing directions or information on the board. Invariably several students would raise their hands happily to correct me. I modeled the appropriate behavior for constructive criticism. We also talked about the possibility of being a "critical" friend who helps us correct ourselves without making us feel bad.

For Cognitive Development

- Play games with open-ended questions.
- Play strategy games such as chess, checkers, etc.
- Encourage memorization of prose and poetry.
- Play 20 Questions: show how to use categorical questions.
- Find simple logic problems for eight-year-olds to solve.
- Use simple Sudoku puzzles.
- Pretest in content areas and differentiate according to interest, readiness, and learning style.

Brain Briefing

The End of Early Childhood: Another Beginning

What will age nine bring? As students approach the "tween" years, there will be new concerns, new friendships, and the beginning of brain and body changes to prepare for adolescence. Many of our students begin puberty at a very young age. With the physical changes comes another proliferation of brain connections. The brain will bloom as new synapses prepare for another sculpting. Adolescence is looming, and with it comes the opportunity to redesign the brain. Experiences are still the important ingredient in changing the brain.

Nutrition also affects this brain growth, and nine-year-olds may desire junk food. It is a time of modeling the importance of healthy foods and adequate sleep.

Nine-year-olds will realize that adults in authority are not always right. Friendships, clubs, and cliques begin to develop at this age. The frontal lobe has developed during the first eight years, and it is at a point where nine-year-olds may be able to better control their anger. That frontal lobe, however, has a long way to go for full maturity. The end of early childhood marks the beginning of middle childhood, when students take more responsibility for actions and learning.

Child Development Checklist: Eight-Year-Olds

Name _____ Grade _____

Birth date _____ Chronological Age _____

LANGUAGE and READING DEVELOPMENT

____ Replaces learning to read with reading to learn

____ Can relate rather involved accounts of events, many from the past

____ Uses complex and compound sentences easily

____ Usually has few lapses in grammatical constructions

____ Has established all speech sounds, including consonant blends

____ Can read with considerable ease and now write simple compositions

____ Can use social amenities in speech in appropriate situations

____ Can control rate, pitch, and volume when reading aloud

____ Can carry on conversation at a rather adult level

____ Follows fairly complex directions with little repetition

Recommendations for increasing reading and language growth:

_____

_____

_____

PHYSICAL and MOTOR DEVELOPMENT

____ Wiggles and clowns around

____ Makes faces

____ May have accidents due to so much activity

____ Needs physical activity every day, approximately 30 minutes

____ Team sports are important. Emphasis must be based on exercise, social interaction, and having a good time rather than competition.

____ Perform in much the same way as a seven-year-old; see checklist in previous chapter

Recommendations for increasing physical and motor growth:

_____

_____

_____

SOCIAL and EMOTIONAL GROWTH

____ Articulates feelings

____ Tends to dramatize

____ Eventually obeys, but may begin with resistance

____ Likes instant gratification and positive reinforcement

____ Usually is affectionate, helpful, cheerful, outgoing, and curious

____ Can also be rude, demanding, silly, and bossy

____ Makes new friends easily; works at establishing good two-way relationships

____ May develop close friend of own sex

____ Considers clubs and groups important

____ Enjoys school, doesn't like to be absent, and tends to talk more about it

____ Is somewhat possessive of his or her things

____ May keep secrets

____ May be sensitive

Recommendations for increasing social and emotional growth:

_____

_____

_____

COGNITIVE GROWTH

____ Wants to know the reasons for things

____ Can retell a story with events in the right order

____ Begins to find math useful

____ Needs skills and rituals that lay a solid base for moving on to new challenges

____ Sees many points of view

____ Realizes that doing well depends on paying attention

____ Has well developed time and number concepts

Recommendations for increasing cognitive growth:

_____

_____

_____

Bibliography

Altmann, T. (Editor-in-chief). (2006). *The wonder years.* New York: Bantam.

Amen, D. (2006, January). *Healing ADD: See and heal the six types of ADD.* Presentation at the Learning Brain Expo. San Diego CA.

Armistead, V., Duke, N., & Moses, A. (2005). *Literacy and the youngest learner.* New York: Scholastic.

Barnet, A. B., & Barnet, R. J. (1988). *The youngest minds, parenting & genes in the development of intellect & emotion.* New York: Simon & Schuster.

Begley, S. (2007). *Train your brain, change your mind.* New York: Ballantine Books.

Bergen, D. (2006). Early childhood. In S. Feinstein (Ed.), *The Praeger handbook of learning and the brain* (pp. 187–192). Westport, CT: Praeger.

Bergen, D., & Coscia, J. (2001). *Brain research and childhood education: Implications for educators.* Olney, MD: Association for Childhood Education International.

Berger, A., Tzur, G., & Posner, M. (2006). Infant brains detect arithmetic errors. *Proceedings of the National Academy of Sciences, 103*(33), 12,649–12,653 .

Berk, L. (2006). *Child development* (7th ed.). New York: Pearson.

Brookes, C. (2006, January). *Teaching literacy with the young brain in mind.* Presentation at the Learning Brain Expo, San Diego, CA.

Bruer, J. (2002). *The myth of the first three years.* New York: Free Press.

Campbell, F. A., Ramey, C. T., Pungello, E. P., Sparling, J., & Miller-Johnson, S. (2002). Early childhood education: Young adult outcomes from the Abecedarian Project. *Applied Developmental Science, 6,* 42–57.

Carey, J. (Ed.). (2005*). Brain facts. A primer on the brain and nervous system.* Washington DC: Society for Neuroscience.

Carlson, N. (1988). *I like me.* New York: Viking Kestrel.

Casey, B. J., Giedd, J. N., & Thomas, K. M. (2000). Structural and functional brain development and its relation to cognitive development. *Biological Psychology, 54,* 241–257.

Certain, L., & Kahn, R. S. (2002). Prevalence, correlates, and trajectory of television viewing among infants and toddlers. *Pediatrics, 109*(4), 634–642.

Chugani, H. (1999). PET scanning studies of human brain development and plasticity. *Developmental Neuropsychology, 16*(3), 379–381.

Diamond, M., & Hopson, J. (1998). *Magic trees of the mind.* New York: Penguin.

Dodge, D., & Heroman, C. (1999). *Building your baby's brain: A parent's guide to the first five years.* Washington, DC: Teaching Strategies.

Dowling, M. (2005). *Young children's personal, social, and emotional development* (2nd ed.). London: Paul Chapman.

Eide, B. & Eide, F. (2006). *The mislabeled child.* New York: Hyperion.

Elias, M., & Arnold, H. (Eds.). (2006). *The educator's guide to emotional intelligence and academic achievement.* Thousand Oaks, CA: Corwin Press.

Eliot, L. (1999). *What's going on in there? How the brain and mind develop in the first five years.* New York: Bantam Books.

Eliot, L. (2006). Infant brain. In S. Feinstein (Ed.), *The Praeger handbook of learning and the brain* (pp. 251–255). Westport, CT: Praeger.

Eliot, L. (2007, April). *What's going on in there? Nature, nurture and early brain development.* Presentation at Learning and the Brain Conference, Cambridge, MA.

Fields, D., & Brown, A. (2006). *Toddler 411.* Boulder, CO: Windsor Peak Press.

Fox, M. (2001). *Reading magic.* San Diego, CA: Harcourt.

Giedd, J., Thompson, P., Woods, R., MacDonald, D., Evans, A., & Toga, A. (2000). Growth patterns in the developing brain detected by using continuum mechanical tensor maps. *Nature, 404,* 190–193.

Ginsburg, K., Committee on Communications, & Committee on Psychosocial Aspects of Child and Family Health. (2007). Clinical report: The importance of play in promoting healthy development and maintaining strong parent-child bonds. *Pediatrics, 119*(1), 182–191.

Goleman, D. (1995). *Emotional intelligence.* New York: Bantam.

Goleman, D. (1998). *Working with emotional intelligence.* New York: Bantam.

Goleman, D., Boyatzis, R., & McKee. A. (2002). *Primal leadership.* Boston: Harvard Business School Press.

Goodwyn, S., Acredolo, L., & Brown, C. (2000). Impact of symbolic gesturing on early language development. *Journal of Nonverbal Behavior, 24*(2), 81–103.

Gopnik, A., Meltzoff, A. N., & Kuhl, P. K. (1999). *The scientist in the crib: What early learning tells us about the mind.* New York: William Morrow.

Greenough, W. T. , Black, J. E., & Wallace, C. S. (1987). Experience and brain development. *Child Development, 58,* 539–559.

Grusec, J. E., Goodnow, J. J., & Cohen, L. (1997). Household work and the development of children's concern for others. *Developmental Psychology, 32,* 999–1000.

Gurian, M. (2007). *Nurture the nature.* San Francisco: Jossey-Bass.

Hannaford, C. (2005). *Smart moves* (2nd ed.). Salt Lake City, UT: Great Rivers Books.

Hart, B., & Risley, T. (1995). *Meaningful differences.* Baltimore: Paul Brookes.

Healy, J. (2004). *Your child's growing mind.* New York: Broadway.

Herr, J., & Larson, Y. (2004). *Creative resources for the early childhood classroom* (4th ed.). Clifton Park, NY: Delmar Learning.

Herschkowitz, N., & Herschkowitz, E. (2002). *A good start in life.* Washington, DC: Joseph Henry Press.

Herschkowitz, N. & Herschkowitz, E. (2006, May). *Intense Brain Development Between Four & Eight Years and its Impact on Preschool & School Years.* Presentation at Learning and the Brain Conference, Cambridge, MA.

Hirsh-Pasek, K., & Golinkoff, R. (2003). *Einstein never used flash cards.* Emmaus, PA: Rodale.

Jacobs, G., & Crowley, K. (2007). *Play, projects, and preschool standards.* Thousand Oaks, CA: Corwin Press.

Jensen, E. (2005). *Teaching with the brain in mind.* Alexandria, VA: Association for Supervision and Curriculum Development.

Jordan, K., & Brannon, E. (2006). The multisensory representation of number in infancy. *Proceedings of the National Academy of Sciences, 103*(9), 3,486–3,489.

Kagan, J., & Herschkowitz, N. (2005). *A young mind in a growing brain.* Mahwah, NJ: Lawrence Erlbaum.

Kaltman, G. (2006). *More help for teachers of young children.* Thousand Oaks, CA: Corwin Press.

Linden, D. (2007). *The accidental mind.* Cambridge, MA: The Belknap Press of Harvard University.

Maclean, M., Bryant, P., & Bradley, L. (1987). Rhymes, nursery rhymes, and reading in early childhood. *Merrill-Palmer Quarterly, 33*(3), 255–281.

Marzano, R., Pickering, D., & Pollack, J. (2001). *Classroom instruction that works.* Alexandria, VA: Association for Supervision and Curriculum Development.

McCormick Tribune Foundation (Producer). (2004). *Ten things every child needs* [DVD]. Chicago: Chicago Production Center.

National Association for the Education of Young Children. (1996). *Principles of child development and learning that inform developmentally appropriate practice.* Retrieved October 30, 2007, from http://www.naeyc.org/about/positions/dap3.asp

Paus, T., Collins, D. L., Evans, A. C., Leonard, G., Pike, B., & Zijdenbos, A. (2001). Maturation of white matter in the human brain: A review of magnetic resonance studies. *Brain Research Bulletin, 54,* 255–266.

Perry, B., & Szalavitz, M. (2007). *The boy who was raised by a dog.* New York: Basic Books.

Peterson, S. (2001). *How the young brain learns. Tape 2: The nature of the young brain* [Audiotape]. Alexandria, VA: Association for Supervision and Curriculum Development.

Public Broadcasting System. (2002–2007). *Does the American Academy of Pediatrics recommend against TV viewing for children under the age of 2?* Retrieved October 17, 2007, from http://www.pbs.org/parents/childrenandmedia/article-faq.html#americanacademy

Rodriguez, A. (2007). *A day in the life of the brain.* New York: Chelsea House.

Ross, R., & Pachione, B. (2007). *Wanna play?* Thousand Oaks, CA: Corwin Press.

Schaefer, C. & DiGeronimo, T. (2000). *Ages and stages.* New York: Wiley.

Schmithorst, V. J., Wilke, M., Dardzinski, B. J., & Holland, S. K. (2002). Correlation of white matter diffusivity and anisotropy with age during childhood and adolescence: A cross-sectional diffusion-tensor MR imaging study. *Radiology, 222,* 212–218.

Shaywitz, S. (2003). *Overcoming dyslexia.* New York: Alfred Knopf.

Shevlov, S. (Ed.). (2004). *Caring for your baby and young child birth to five.* Elk Grove Village, IL: American Academy of Pediatrics.

Shonkoff, J. P. (2000). *From neurons to neighborhoods: The science of early childhood development.* Washington, DC: National Academy Press.

Shore, R. (2003). *Rethinking the brain.* New York: Families and Work Institute.

Siegel, D. (1999). *The developing mind.* New York: Guilford Press.

Siegel, D. (2007, February). *The developing mind: How emotions and relationships shape child development.* Presentation at Learning and the Brain conference, San Francisco, CA.

Sleeper, A. (2007). *Speech and language.* New York: Chelsea House.

Sousa, D. (2006). *How the brain learns* (3rd ed.). Thousand Oaks, CA: Corwin Press.

Sprenger, M. (1999). *Learning and memory: The brain in action.* Alexandria, VA: Association for Supervision and Curriculum Development.

Sprenger, M. (2006). *Memory 101 for educators.* Thousand Oaks, CA: Corwin Press.

Sprenger, M. (2007). *Becoming a "wiz" at brain-based teaching.* Thousand Oaks, CA: Corwin Press.

Stamm, J., & Spencer, P. (2007). *Bright from the start.* New York: Gotham Books.

Sunderland, M. (2006). *The science of parenting.* New York: DK.

Sylwester, R. (2003). *A biological brain in a cultural classroom.* Thousand Oaks, CA: Corwin Press.

Sylwester, R. (2007). *The adolescent brain.* Thousand Oaks, CA: Corwin Press.

Tallal, P. (2007, March). *Better living through neuroscience.* Presentation at the annual conference of the Association for Supervision and Curriculum Development, Anaheim, CA.

Trelease, J. (2001). *The read-aloud handbook* (5th ed.). New York: Penguin Books.

Wesson, K. (2005, July). *Scientific teaching: Merging brain science with the classroom.* Presentation at the Learning Brain Expo, Austin, TX.

Willis, J. (2006). *Research-based strategies to ignite student learning.* Alexandria, VA: Association for Supervision and Curriculum Development.

Wood, C. (1997). *Yardsticks.* Turners Falls, MA: Northeast Foundation for Children.

Woodfield, L. (2004). *Physical development in the early years.* New York: Continuum.

Index

CORWIN PRESS

The Corwin Press logo—a raven striding across an open book—represents the union of courage and learning. Corwin Press is committed to improving education for all learners by publishing books and other professional development resources for those serving the field of PreK–12 education. By providing practical, hands-on materials, Corwin Press continues to carry out the promise of its motto: **"Helping Educators Do Their Work Better."**